LEADERS OF THE PACK

PACK

and the FUTURE of VETERINARY MEDICINE

NEW DIRECTIONS IN THE HUMAN-ANIMAL BOND
Series editors Alan M. Beck and Marguerite E. O'Haire

LEADERS OF THE PACK

WOMEN and the FUTURE of VETERINARY MEDICINE

JULIE KUMBLE and DONALD F. SMITH

Purdue University Press / West Lafayette, Indiana

Cataloging-in-Publication Data available at the Library of Congress.

Paperback ISBN: 978-1-55753-772-0
ePub ISBN: 978-1-61249-487-6
ePDF ISBN: 978-1-61249-486-9

Cover credit: Micha Archer

Contents

Acknowledgments

We are indebted to the women and men whose stories told in this book personify leadership and instruct future leaders that rather than a pinnacle, leadership is a sequence of decisions based on optimism and courage. We thank the staff, senior officers, and members of the AVMA Board and House of Delegates—in particular Drs. Janet Donlin, Beth Sabin, Ted Cohn, Jan Krehbiel, Anna Reddish, and Caroline Cantner. Thanks to Dr. Linda Tintle, with whom we had one of our earliest conversations about women's leadership; Dr. Doug Aspros, who emerged early as a colleague committed to doing something lasting; Dr. Karen Bradley, who put her energy into the Women's Veterinary Leadership Development Initiative (WVLDI) and brought us along on her journey; past and current WVLDI board members; Dr. Christine Navarre and board members of the North American Veterinary Community; Dr. Joni Samuels and board members of the Western Veterinary Conference; Drs. Laura Molgaard, Bob Lester, John Weale, Jenny Sones, and Raphael Malbrue; the generous staff at Banfield; Drs. Bonnie Beaver, Beth Leininger, Kate Hodgson, and Dean Eleanor Green; Erin Eldermere at Cornell University Veterinary Library; Drs. Andrew Maccabe, Lisa Greenhill, and others at the Association of American Veterinary Medical Colleges; Dean Tim Ogilvie and Cathy Wybern at St. George's University; Dr. Carmen Fuentealba at Ross University; Dr. Susan Wylegala of the New York State Veterinary Medical Society; Drs. Rebecca Donnelly and David Seader, now new doctors of veterinary medicine; Drs. Sarah Peters, Andrea Dennis-LaVigne, Renee Bayha Gossett, Marike Visser, and Barbara Bucki-Ohm; and Amy Pollock, MD. Thanks to faculty and staff at Purdue University, including Dean Willie Reed, Drs. Kauline Davis, Tina Tran, Laurie Jaeger, Susan Mendrysa, Alan Beck, and Maggie O'Haire. Thank-you to Purdue University Press staff, especially Peter Froehlich and Katherine Purple, for their support throughout.

We especially appreciate all the students who contributed their insights at universities, including Cornell, Iowa State, Tufts, Ross, St. George's, Purdue, Virginia–Maryland, Louisiana State, Auburn, Lincoln Memorial, Minnesota and the Student American Veterinary Medical Association (SAVMA) Symposium. Finally, we thank the veterinarians and technicians who offered their time, professional perspectives, and personal kindness during the hours of interviews and reviews.

Julie gives special thanks to my dear friend, Don Smith, who made this journey possible and positively life changing. I'm also grateful for the veterinarians throughout the country who welcomed me into the profession in countless ways; Carla Oleska, friend, mentor and the ultimate servant-leader; Micha Archer for her cover art and friendship; Emily Monosson for regular walks and occasional reviews; my supportive siblings and parents; and my friends who make western Massachusetts home. Thanks to Jackson for his relentless enthusiasm and our daily romps. Special acknowledgments to Elena and Nate for being the foundation of everything, and to Bruce, ultimately, for his exacting edits and constant support.

Don is grateful for the support of the faculty and administration of the Cornell University College of Veterinary Medicine for providing an academic home for over three decades; also to the students who over the years have been a great source of inspiration and pride. To the women in my life: my mother, who understood equanimity; my daughter Debra and her growing Abby, who just "do it"; to newer daughters Corey and Rachel, who add joy and belonging; and to Doris, who understands the critical nature of leadership in herself and others.

Author's Note

Donald F. Smith passed away on October 29, 2016. Just days before he became ill, we submitted the manuscript to this book. Despite the profound loss, I take comfort that he experienced the joy of seeing the work to fruition, from our earliest conversations to the cover design. This project was but one of many distinguished achievements within the bookends of a remarkable life. With his passing, the veterinary profession has lost a giant.

Those who knew Don were fortunate to enjoy his generous, warm, and expansive spirit. He loved learning about people from all backgrounds and especially loved encouraging students, colleagues, and friends to find their paths, often ones he illuminated for them. "He believed in me before I believed in myself," say many who knew him.

Don's journey took him from a childhood on an Ontario dairy farm to his extraordinary career as a leading authority on bovine surgery. Along the way, he earned his Doctor of Veterinary Medicine from Guelph University, graduating with distinction, completed a residency in large animal surgery at the University of Pennsylvania, became a diplomate of the American College of Veterinary Surgeons, and served for ten years (1997–2007) as dean of the Cornell University College of Veterinary Medicine. His research on metabolic alkalosis in ruminants was instrumental in advancing the field of metabolic diseases of cattle.

Don delighted in the stories of veterinary leaders past and present. His passion for history resulted in a popular veterinary history course at Cornell as well as his *Veterinary Legacy* blog (www.veterinarylegacy.blogspot.com) that is still read across the world and is considered a treasure trove of the profession's history and commentary on prevailing issues in veterinary medicine. In 2015, he authored *Pathways to Progress*, a history of the veterinary colleges in the United States and beyond.

Don was an ardent champion of women in leadership, and he researched, taught, and spoke forcefully about the need for women to direct veterinary medicine to keep the profession thriving. It was in this arena that we became colleagues. Don was known for his curiosity and genuine interest in people, and I was fortunate to be one of those he met, quite by chance. He was a generous professional, introducing me to the history, challenges, triumphs, and leaders in veterinary medicine. I shared my perspectives of gender barriers and successes in women's issues. Despite vastly different careers, our professional collaboration grew, always in a spirit of exploration, lively debate, and a commitment to women's leadership. In the four and half years since we met, we shared an intensity in purpose, researching leadership issues and examining data. In that period, we interviewed hundreds of individuals, wrote over 30 online articles, developed a course at Cornell, taught educators at other universities how to tailor leadership courses for their own students, delivered seminars at conferences and universities, and wrote this book.

What began as an unanticipated professional partnership became a cherished friendship. It is a rare thing to develop an unlikely bond, and I'm blessed by that gift. Four and a half years is brutally short, and yet I'm grateful beyond words for knowing Don. His kindness, generosity, and encouragement far surpassed his grand achievements. In an era where cynicism is chic, Don was unabashedly effusive. He told people he considered special—ranging from janitors to colleagues of high rank—that he loved them. His wife, Doris, and their children and grandchildren were blessed by those qualities during his lifetime. It is those qualities above all that I hope to carry forth to continue his legacy and remain in his bright realm.

In cowriting *Leaders of the Pack*, Don's favorite chapter to work on was "For the Greater Good" because it celebrated people who embodied the principle of servant-leadership. Don was one of the true, great servant-leaders in his beloved veterinary profession and in women's leadership. May his spirit and dedication live on.

Julie Kumble
December 2016

Introduction

From dog dentist to dean, the image of a veterinary leader is different for all of us. I might picture a laboratory pathologist deep into her research while you imagine a board-certified equine surgeon who also directs her multi-doctor practice like NASA ground control. Someone else envisions a public health officer tracking an avian influenza outbreak, while yet another thinks of a practice associate who is the consummate community member, volunteering as a 4-H leader, and working with the county health commissioner to develop criteria so that the local hospital administrator can legally allow pets in recovery rooms. The notion of a leader is tied less to title and position than to influence and impact.

While our idea of leaders is as varied as we are, one persistent image that seems grafted into our minds is that of the person who forges ahead with inspired followers in tow. For those raised on movies where leaders are solitary cowboys, tough military brass, or barking business tycoons, the image is decidedly individualistic, authoritative, and male.

Today, we know better because we've seen more. Leadership demands a wide range of skills, and while being solitary and tough can serve us well, so does being deliberative and collaborative. In veterinary medicine, the massive influx of women into the profession together with the unique qualities and aspirations of today's generation entering the field, call for a broader mindset and skillset.

The transformative entrance of women into the profession began in the 1970s, when legal and cultural changes ushered a wider acceptance of women as doctors. The seismic shifts came in the 1980s when women entering veterinary colleges reached 50 percent, and again in 2007 when the number of women in the entire professional workforce surpassed men.

While women now comprise about 55 percent of all veterinarians, leaders who hold top positions, from practice owners to industry CEOs to deans of veterinary colleges and directors in organized veterinary medicine, are comprised on average of only 25 percent women. This leadership gap isn't unique to veterinary medicine; in fact, according to researchers on economics, politics, education, and culture, the leadership gap exists everywhere, even in prototypically female professions like nursing and nonprofit service. For most professions, women hold an average of just 20 percent of top positions. In Congress, it's still under 20 percent. It would seem, therefore, that veterinary medicine at 25 percent is doing quite well. It *is* thriving in many respects, but because the demographics of students and practicing veterinarians tilt so heavily toward women, the gender gap is acutely noticeable and problematic. Why, then, is the profession still imbalanced?

One reason top positions are still held by men is that they once made up the majority in the profession and therefore naturally ascended to those leadership posts, positions that they still occupy. Women simply haven't caught up. But in many parts of the country, women have comprised over half of the graduating veterinarians for well over three decades and there's still a shortage of women at top levels.

The causes of the very real leadership gap between women and men are complex, multifactorial, and stubbornly embedded in our mentalities, cultural norms, and social policies. Most of us want a society at large and a profession in particular that reflect our demographics, but because of the stew of cultural, systemic, psychological, and economic factors, we just can't seem to accelerate progress. Or can we?

There isn't one single cause of the gender gap, nor one gleaming solution. If that was the case, we'd be a lot closer to closing it and we wouldn't be writing this book. Through over two hundred interviews and related research, what's clear is that an abundance of men and women care deeply about shifting the leadership of the profession to reflect the growing numbers of women, and they're working hard to bring about change. People as diverse as the self-proclaimed "old white men" of the American Veterinary Medical Association (AVMA), leaders of the Student AVMA (SAVMA), and deans at veterinary colleges are all focused on women's leadership. In the following pages, we tease apart the challenges and offer solutions to help bring greater balance to the leadership in veterinary medicine. Our goal isn't just to promote women's leadership for it's own sake, but to ensure that the multibillion-dollar veterinary industry is led mostly by veterinarians.

The plethora of books, workshops, conferences, and institutes dedicated to leadership all point to people's understandable desire to fulfill their potential and realize their ambitions. The problem is that most of the leadership proponents suggest that the same framework and skills can be applied in settings as diverse as nonprofits, nursing, sports, or medicine. Most leadership approaches take a general view, often drawn from the business milieu, and apply it to complex, specific situations.

We firmly believe that some of the most effective solutions come from cross-professional approaches, and we promote learning and collaborating from within and outside veterinary medicine. As coauthors from different backgrounds, we embody this very principle, and we debate, agree, and differ, all in the spirit of learning. However, for this book we have drawn most of our examples and recommendations from the veterinary profession. We've examined the leadership research in veterinary medicine, limited as it is, and have conducted hours of interviews with veterinarians—mostly women but also many men—in order to offer veterinary-specific leadership strategies.

Another limitation in most of the leadership literature and development methods, in our opinion, is that they focus on helping individuals achieve success much more than promoting solutions that would benefit greater numbers of people. Some leadership research and practice suggest that women might have interests beyond their salaries or benefits, such as better family leave policies, flexible schedules, or more time for community service, but those approaches rarely emphasize collective action as a goal other than in passing. Their enthusiastic focus on individual advancement diverts instruction on how people could, and should, work toward organizational and societal reform. In a world where pathogens travel across borders as quickly as jets can carry them, where zoonotic problems call for One Health solutions, and where human health can be vastly improved by creative applications of the human-animal bond, we need leaders whose views and skills target broad solutions that benefit society. Fortunately, some of the most socially focused leadership training is found in organized veterinary medicine at all levels—local associations, state groups, and the AVMA—and many, many members are leading the charge to improve society.

We deeply value leadership for the greater good, naming our final chapter for this principle. We also value leadership for people's sense of personal satisfaction and wellness. We explore the intricate balance of leadership, success, and happiness in one of our chapters, and firmly believe that leadership aspirations shouldn't become another pressure point for veterinarians at the expense of happiness and well-being. The disturbing fact is that veterinary medicine has a suicide rate higher than all other professions, and we are emphatic that aspiring to leadership should enhance people's joy, satisfaction, and connection to others.

Do we need to ask if veterinarians gravitate toward leadership literature and programs that promote individual success over collective change? Are veterinarians more oriented to animals than people and therefore are less likely to engage in policy activities that involve debate, compromise, and committees? Some research suggests that women in general don't identify as a particularly oppressed class of people;[1] therefore, are female veterinarians even less likely to see themselves as a group that should organize to pursue shared goals? None of these suggestions is backed by research, but the questions are worth exploring because they offer insight into how we have gotten here and how we will move forward.

We do know that generational differences play a role in how women do or do not get involved in social change. For the most part, the early trailblazers were outliers with different qualities than the broad swath of women who today make up the majority of the profession and veterinary colleges. Some female veterinarians who succeeded in the early days and became leaders were reluctant to take on "women's issues" because they didn't want to be branded as difficult or as "angry feminists," fearing they might jeopardize their own paths. Or because they made it in a man's world, they believe that young women who are coming up today have it much easier and do not need special championing. Younger veterinarians haven't experienced the obstacles, subtle and blatant, of their predecessors, and they are less likely to take up the mantle of leadership, at first. Or they themselves do not want the attention of being labeled a feminist.

Fourth-year Cornell veterinary student Michelle Forella says of the Women's Veterinary Leadership Development Initiative (WVLDI), "I had heard about WVLDI before, but didn't think much about it much because it had 'the W word' and I was still afraid of that stigma. When we had the women's leadership course in March 2014, it was eye-opening to learn that women in veterinary medicine still face obstacles. Still, if it wasn't for the camaraderie I felt when discussing these challenges openly with my classmates, I wouldn't have felt as empowered to champion women's leadership going forward."

Through camaraderie or a sense of passing along opportunities, many women who are in leadership, older and younger, have used their prospects and sense of obligation to promote changes that make leadership more accessible to others. In the pages of this book, we ardently support women and men in veterinary medicine who are working together for improved policies that help women succeed and achieve leadership, and we feature their stories and strategies for improving the profession.

Well over 80 percent of clients who take their companion animals to a veterinary clinic are women themselves,[2] and they are fascinated by the stories of the female doctors managing their pets' health. As animal lovers, many once considered becoming veterinarians. Ask people about their vet and they're likely to speak glowingly. In writing this book, when we shared our project with friends and strangers, nearly everyone enthusiastically said the same thing: "You should interview my vet! She's so smart and caring."

The individuals profiled in these pages reflect multiple sectors of the profession. Some will be recognized as high-profile leaders, while others are influencing veterinary medicine in ways that haven't garnered press releases but are nevertheless bold and authentic. There are far too many outstanding people in the profession to ever fit between the covers of one book, and we chose to highlight individuals who demonstrate qualities and life paths rather than hold them up as "best" examples. As diverse as the people and their stories are, the common characteristic is their commitment to advancing our profession.

Change at top levels will eventually come about as more and more women enter the profession, many say, but because leadership posts are still predominantly male after so many years of women outnumbering men, we can't just be patient and wait. Simply speaking, it's unfair to the current generation to be patient and wait for seats to open at the top. We risk losing out on their full range of talents by asking them to wait or to deal with the array of hurdles that we can minimize.

Among the changes that can't wait for gradual implementation are:

- Changing organizational policies to better accommodate women's different career paths, their multiple work and life goals, and the reality that they bear children and, still, do the majority of household work in couples;
- Closing the salary gap between men and women by researching the various causes and by developing targeted strategies;
- Reducing women's psychological barriers to self-advancement through effective and accessible training; and
- Integrating leadership and professional development into veterinary education with the same rigor as clinical training.

If these and possibly other changes were brought to the front burners *now*, wouldn't we encourage a wider swath of talent to move to leadership positions? Imagine how veterinary medicine would shine as a bold exemplar among other professions if its leadership profile more closely reflected the demographics of its own profession. More importantly, with more women in key leadership positions, the very nature of the profession itself—whether the commitment to One Health, serving rural areas at the interface of human and animal health, or a dozen other priorities—might increase its value to society and open up new opportunities for workforce expansion.

What can we anticipate as essential leadership qualities for the future? Forecasted changes in veterinary medicine include growth across the profession, whether through increasing the proportion of owners seeking care for their pets, by harnessing the genome to personalize animal medicine, leveraging the human-animal bond to enhance human health and welfare, adopting the principles of One Health for public health and comparative medicine, corporatization of practices and management, and online teaching and learning for veterinarians and veterinary technologists. Good or bad, the point about these changes is that they're here or just around the corner.

Looking ahead, we might not know everything that will face veterinary medicine, but we know we will need leaders with the sharpest skills honed from the past, an understanding of the profession's history, and the most up-to-date approaches from today to help guide the way.[3] We do not know precisely what the future of the profession will look like, but we know that brilliant and committed students and new veterinarians are ready to take the helm. We should teach what we know, encourage and support them, then stand back and let them lead.

Notes

1.   Barbara Kellerman and Deborah L. Rhode, *Women and Leadership: The State of Play and Strategies for Change* (San Francisco: Wiley and Sons, 2007).

2.   John Payne (former CEO Banfield Pet Hospital), personal communication with authors, March 7, 2016.

3.   James W. Lloyd, Lonnie J. King, Carol A. Mase, and Donna Harris, "Future Needs and Recommendations for Leadership in Veterinary Medicine," *Journal of the American Veterinary Medical Association 226,* no. 7 (2005): 1060–67, http://dx.doi.org/10.2460/javma.2005.226.1060; Karen M. Bradley, Elizabeth M. Charles, and Joan C. Hendricks, "A Renewed Call for Veterinary Leaders," *Journal of the American Veterinary Medical Association 247,* no. 6 (2015): 592–94, http://dx.doi.org/10.2460/javma.247.6.592.

1

Owning It—Passion and Entrepreneurs

Dr. Justine Lee

Walk down the aisle of any airliner and you're likely to see passengers reading everything from *Newsweek* to Tom Clancy, Jane Austen to Stephen King. In 2007, Dr. Justine Lee was on a typical flight, enjoying some light-hearted fare—*Why Do Men Have Nipples? Hundreds of Questions You'd Only Ask a Doctor After Your Third Martini*—and chuckling at the humorous medical advice. Suddenly, encountering some unexpected *personal* turbulence, she put down her book and gripped the armrests. "I could write a version of this best-selling book for pet owners and help animals in a new way," she thought.

Justine wasn't looking for a new project to add to her busy life. She was already an assistant professor in veterinary emergency and critical care (ECC) at the University of Minnesota College of Veterinary Medicine, as well as a practitioner in emergency medicine. She had invested months studying for her American College of Veterinary Emergency Critical Care (ACVECC) boards just four years earlier. Though versed in publishing in peer-reviewed journals for veterinarians, Justine had never published anything for a commercial market, but she knew that a book about the health and behaviors of dogs and cats could help pet owners understand the medical side of their animals. It would improve animal health and maybe even save lives, and it would help pet owners save money by taking care of preventative issues rather than spending thousands in emergency care. Soon after her epiphany at 35,000 feet, Justine wrote *It's a Dog's Life . . . but It's Your Carpet* and *It's a Cat's World . . . You Just Live in It.* Both books were published in 2008 by Crown Publishing, a division of Random House, the same press that had published *Why Do Men Have Nipples?*

People like Justine aren't deterred by the words "You've never done it before." The curious people we call entrepreneurs are used to warnings like, "It's going to take a ton of work and there are no guarantees you'll succeed." But two popular books later, Justine insists that any veterinarian could have written those books. "We often squash the creativity in our brains because we're very scientifically driven," she says. "We all have awesome ideas but very few of us follow through and say, 'You know what, I'm going to do this!'"

Despite the success of Justine's books and teaching career, academics hadn't always been her strength and she'd struggled as a C student in veterinary school. What she had in abundance, though, was energy, passion, and a willingness to work very hard. These innate qualities fuel her and other veterinary entrepreneurs. Other traits—business acumen, social skills, and confidence—can be learned, Justine insists, if veterinarians, especially women, are willing to go for it. The term *sweat equity* constantly bubbles through her comments.

Stress is common in veterinary medicine, and Justine has experienced her share of it through her work in emergency and critical care, where euthanasia is common, economic pressures are great, and the human-animal bond is ever present either as crushing loss or joyous recovery. Add to that pet owners who are stressed emotionally or strapped economically, and the pressures mount for veterinarians. Wellness is a serious concern across the profession, perhaps even more so for driven, go-getters like Justine who experienced burnout and compassion fatigue. In 2008, after eleven years in practice and advanced clinical training, she left veterinary medicine for a new challenge—associate director of an animal and human poison control center where she worked for the next five years.

After a few years spent directing the center, Justine began studying for her second round of boards, this time in toxicology. But just as when she studied for the ECC boards, she felt there could be a better way to maximize her hours and energy. She felt guilty about taking a break from her twelve-hour study day, even for walking the dog or going for a run, and she wished she could listen to a tape of her study topics while multitasking. Once again, she encountered unexpected inner turbulence.

This was the beginning of the golden age of smartphones, podcasts, and online education. Again, Justine was ready. Why not launch a podcast to help veterinarians learn and earn continuing education (CE) credits? Why not allow busy veterinarians to study while driving to work, picking up the kids, or going for that run? The idea was born for VETgirl, a subscription-based podcast and webinar service offering online veterinary CE. She reached out to a tech-savvy veterinarian specialist and colleague Garret Pachtinger, one of the first to have a PalmPilot back when they were state-of-the-art, and she pitched him the idea and asked him to partner in this new IT venture. The two became business partners and launched VETgirl in 2013. Now Justine is its full-time CEO and offers online veterinary CE hours to both national and international audiences. She is also the voice heard on VETgirl, where her speaking voice—precise, warm, and enthusiastic—is pitch perfect for podcasts.

American culture exalts entrepreneurism. We are infused with "roll up the shirtsleeves" and "pull up the bootstraps" stories that convey gutsiness and success. But risk-taking has long been traditionally associated with men rather than women because of gender stereotypes and cultural biases—we encourage boys to take risks and reward our girls for behaving nicely.[1] Whether based in biology, personality, or stereotypes, taking risks is part of what makes a good entrepreneur, and even if some come by it naturally, others certainly can develop the skill. As more women dominate the workforce in veterinary medicine, more will become entrepreneurs.

Are some people born business builders? Can gutsiness be taught? Is risk-taking something that can be learned? Depending on the researchers and their era, responses are different. Today a surplus of how-to business books crowd the shelves. Television channels and airwaves all pitch self-help scenarios based on developing audacious, bold, and risk-taking habits. Twenty years ago researcher Helen Mills asked, "Can entrepreneurship be taught?" Writing in *Canadian Woman Studies*, Mills defined several qualities that help and hinder entrepreneurism in women.[2] Among the qualities Mills found essential were:

- disobedience and a healthy disrespect for rules;
- endurance;
- feminism, or any credo empowering women;
- self-direction;
- responsibility;
- friends/partners to work with and give support;
- a powerful need for independence and self-determination;
- courage;
- a sense of adventure;
- people skills;
- an ability to persuade, sell, negotiate;
- conceptual skills;
- creativity;
- self-help networks with other businesses;
- credit clubs or other innovative financing instruments; and
- financial need.

The qualities Mills viewed as hindering entrepreneurism include shyness, dread of contact with clients, lack of positive attitudes about money, lack of mentoring, and insecurity about finances.

While entrepreneurs were once admired for their drive and exalted for their moxie, today whether discussing their latest idea for expansion or explaining why they were up until 3:00 a.m., many entrepreneurs list passion as their number one quality.[3] *Harvard Business Review* writer Daniel McGinn says that passion along with patience and attunement to the marketplace are the three main ingredients for successful start-up ventures.[4] Researchers at Simmons College Center for Gender in Organizations use the more technical term *entrepreneurial intensity* (EI). In "Toward a New Model of Intentions: The Complexity of Gender,

Cognitive Style, Culture, Social Norms, and Intensity on the Pathway to Entrepreneurship," Simmons authors Jill Kickul and Norris Krueger describe EI as a single-minded focus to work toward the growth of the venture. Having measured EI, Kickul and Krueger insist it can be taught and promoted.[5]

Self-confidence is an essential partner to passion, or EI. According to the Simmons study, the typical linear, analytic style of teaching entrepreneurism is a standard approach that isn't effective for people on the more creative side of the analytic-intuitive continuum. Self-confidence can indeed be taught, but women need to determine their position on the analytic-intuitive continuum and then incorporate experiential, problem-based learning. These recommendations are in line with what the more innovative and prestigious business schools offer.[6]

Katty Kay and Claire Shipman, coauthors of *The Confidence Code: The Science and Art of Self-Assurance—What Women Should Know,*[7] say that confidence isn't just an attitude but more of a life-enabler, turning thoughts into action. While self-confidence can be taught, another quality that sets the natural-born entrepreneurs apart from the crowd is their propensity to say, "Yes, why not? I can do it, and if I can't now, I can learn how to do it." Entrepreneurs seem to possess reserves of passion whereas others need to cultivate their optimism and drive.

Justine exudes passion. In fact, she's a living example of using sweat equity to work hard, calling herself not a workaholic, but a "workafrolic." Hard work and confidence were ingrained from an early age. "My dad is a pastor, the Chinese equivalent of Billy Graham," she says, "so when I'm lecturing to an audience of 400, I draw on what I learned watching my father preach as a child."

With all that passion and confidence, it's no surprise that Justine was an early adopter of social media in the profession. Small wonder that Justine is concerned about veterinarians' slow uptake in this realm. When she graduated in 1997, veterinarians were viewed in a positive light, often cited among the top ten most trusted professionals, according to Justine, but that has changed dramatically. Because veterinarians were very slow to get online and pet bloggers were way ahead, she says that the trust that people had in beloved veterinarians was eroded.

Veterinarians are now trying to catch up technologically and, critically, regain pet owner trust.

"Social media allows everyone to weigh in with opinions and access cheaper medications," she says. "For example, pet owners have been saying for years that a commonly prescribed flea and tick medication seemed to have decreased efficacy. Veterinarians weren't even aware of this as they weren't paying attention to dog blogs." If veterinarians are not careful, says Justine, others—such as dog and cat bloggers—will fill the void with both accurate and inaccurate medical information and leave veterinary medicine behind in keeping pet owners updated with information that's correct.

Justine is a big believer in taking advantage of online classes and free training to build business skills. She urges all veterinarians to get a limited liability corporation (LLC) license to start their own business and to begin thinking like a business owner. Whether it's owning a practice, consulting, or something else, by starting an LLC, she says, "you start to develop the mindset and skillset to becoming more independent and more of a leader. It sounds intimidating, but for $135 you can get your LLC and tax ID number from your state office and be set up to protect yourself against malpractice, but more importantly to think about yourself as a business owner."

Justine has become a trusted personality in the veterinary profession by blending her passion, business skills, and media savvy. She has made VETgirl synonymous with herself; Justine *is* VETgirl. Because of VETgirl and Justine's example of taking ownership of her career, she'll inspire future veterinary professionals to build their businesses and leadership.

Dr. Jane Brunt

A woman of an earlier generation who also kindled her passion and business interests, Dr. Jane Brunt is one of the best-known and trusted feline specialists in the country. As with most entrepreneurs, she didn't start out that way.

Jane owes her feline expertise to a mouse tale. During her first year of college as a pre-vet student, she was at the livestock fairgrounds participating in Kansas State University's Little American Royal livestock show. A New Jersey girl who hadn't gotten into the eastern vet schools of her choice, she cried when her parents dropped her off on the big, open campus of Kansas State University in Manhattan, Kansas. Feeling alienated in a land where people spoke in flat accents and chewed tobacco, Jane had to summon her inner nerve. Now she stood in the Weber Arena at KSU's College of Agriculture, ready to show the yearling Hereford heifer that she had been working with for weeks. Lead and groom, feed and break, every day until the show.

A cowboy who was readying the pen tossed aside a bale of hay and, seeing a nest of tiny, hairless mice, stomped on them. Though the cowboy saw those mice as vermin, Jane saw them as baby creatures and was horrified; however, the Jersey girl grew up fast that day. The stomped mice steeled her nerves, her heifer won second place, and her parents who had made the trip for her first competition basked in pride. She stuck it out at the Kansas vet school and eventually came to deeply value the midwestern ways, including the work ethic of farmers on call every hour of every day, the ranches measured in sections, and the fried oysters from farms rather than the ocean.

Jane's mother had started a career in medical technology, but she later became a stay-at-home mom with four children, all daughters. She valued and supported girls in science. Jane's father had always wanted to be a veterinarian, but he was denied admittance to the veterinary school at the University of Pennsylvania because he lacked farm experience, so he walked across the street, applied to the medical school, and became a psychiatrist. Jane realizes that her father might have lived some of his earlier dreams through her when she went off to the study veterinary medicine.

Jane stayed at KSU for seven years, earning her undergraduate degree, DVM, and many deep friendships and mentors. Her interest in cats was kindled by one of those mentors. Dr. Russ Frey taught nutrition, and Jane chose feline nutrition as her sophomore project. Two years later, during one of her fourth-year clinics, an intern allowed her to place an IV catheter in a sick cat. Despite the challenge, Jane deftly inserted the tricky catheter, earning recognition from the clinician. "That was a pivotal moment for me," Jane says. "Somebody let me do something and recognized my accomplishment—it became a seed that grew."

Jane's confidence continued from then on. When she graduated, she moved back East and joined a mixed animal practice in Maryland where she worked with cats and dogs at the clinic next to the owner's home and handled farm calls from his station wagon. Her Midwest experience prepared her for the dairy work, and she remembers treating a postpartum cow with a prolapsed uterus by the light of headlights—lifting the rear end of the cow, picking the straw off the mucosa, and massaging the uterus back into its proper place. It was a busy practice and she was left to do a lot on her own. "I knew I *could* do it—farm calls and that lifestyle—and I learned independence," she says. "But I learned I didn't have to have that lifestyle." After a year she moved to a five-doctor cat and dog practice in Baltimore that shared emergency duty before the days of emergency clinics. Weekly calls for cats and dogs were a better fit.

Some people view cats as aloof but she saw their different personalities and behaviors, and she liked the challenge of diagnostics in this quiet, mysterious species. And her feline skills had grown since the deft catheterizing in vet school. Cats were, and still are, an underserved population, and she realized that she could tap the market and work with the species more suited to her. Her entrepreneurism found its outlet.

Starting her own feline practice didn't seem so daunting; she just went ahead and did it. "I wish I had been more analytic than anecdotal about it," she laughs. "I did some shoe-leather market research before deciding on an area for the practice. I went to grocery stores and asked about the cat food and litter sales to determine the potential in the area. Then I colored in a zoning map with the areas that had good visibility and that were appropriately zoned for a veterinary hospital." She found a spot and secured a small business loan and a loan from her parents totaling $60,000.

Being four years out of school and a new owner of a feline practice didn't seem at the time like an achievement based on ambition. "I never consciously thought 'I'm a doer or I'm driven,'" she notes. Jane knows now, from behavior and personality assessments like Myers-Briggs, DiSC, and others, that she is indeed driven and directive. Today, of course, it's called being passionate.

Her breezy description of starting out hides the fact that young vets typically emerge into a business environment very different than the one she found. She admits that students now are much more encumbered by debt and can't be as flexible and perhaps unmethodical as she was when she started her practice. "I did have a business plan but it wasn't a barrier to taking out a business loan," Jane recalls. "I was fortunate not to have student loans. I went to school during the times of state contracts and tuition was less than $1,000 per semester, plus modest living expenses." She's emphatic, though, that young people and associates today can become owners. "They have to be intentional and smart about business and lifestyle choices," she says, echoing Justine Lee's call for launching the business owner mentality early.

Despite the freedom from debt, few female veterinarians of Jane's time opened their own practices so soon after graduation. Her first practice was called the Cat Hospital of Towson (CHAT), the first feline-exclusive practice in the state, which she still owns. She hired her first associate four years later. Initially, she rented her location and in five years purchased a building two miles down the road with better visibility where her practice remains today. Eight years after opening her first clinic, Jane wanted to open a second hospital in a separate area. She opened the Cat Hospital Eastern Shore (CHES), located an hour from CHAT, and sold it to an associate about eight years later.

Like all entrepreneurs, Jane sees a niche and fills it, but her dedication of years in service sets her apart. Parallel to her rapid rise as Maryland's first feline practice owner, she became well-known in organized veterinary medicine, participating extensively in her state association, the American Veterinary Medical Association, the American Animal Hospital Association, and the American Academy of Feline Practitioners, including roles as president and serving on more than fifteen advisory councils. Nationally recognized as one of the eminent feline experts and advocates, she was chair of the CATalyst Summit in 2008 and today serves as executive director of the CATalyst Council, a nonprofit coalition with partners from veterinary medicine, shelter/animal welfare, foundations, industry, and media.

Jane's service to veterinary medicine grew from childhood lessons watching her father, a medical director of a state psychiatric hospital who was active in local and national associations. Her mother helped form the American Psychiatric Association (APA) Auxiliary, and she and her father went to all sorts of meetings, developing lifelong friends around the country. "I'd help my father get ready for those meetings and shine his shoes for him, earning ten cents a pair, and he always brought something home from his trip for me," she remembers. "The annual American Psychiatric Association Convention was something we could count on every May."

That family passion, commitment to professional association service, and understanding of the importance of mental health and well-being has led Jane to start the *Zoë and Harry Brunt Veterinary Medical Student Mental Health and Emotional Well-Being Endowed Fund* at the Kansas State University College of Veterinary Medicine.

In 2007 when she was recognized as an alumni fellow by her alma mater and the KSU Veterinary Medical Alumni Association, Jane gave a talk called "Balance Your Talents." She shared her life wisdom that having "too many windows open can make you feel like you're doing too many things at once. Just like on your computer, when too many windows are open, the system will crash." In life, she said, it's better to have a select number of windows open at a time, and handle them well.

Jane has kept more windows open than most of us, leading the feline world that she loves so much. A self-proclaimed type A personality, learning life lessons and developing a wide array professional leadership skills have gotten her far, but there is no doubt that her warmth, integrity, and generosity—call it midwestern kindness—is at the core of her success.

Dr. Michelle Lem

Many entrepreneurs turn out to be leaders in their profession. The same energy that builds confidence and a desire to work very hard often gets aimed at endeavors beyond their business. Many, like Jane Brunt, also make it a lifelong practice to volunteer services to their profession. For Michelle Lem, entrepreneurism and service are entirely fused. As a social entrepreneur,[8] someone who directs her innovative spirit toward positive community change, it may not be surprising that Michelle heard her call to service in a church.

It was Christmas break during her fourth year of vet school, and Michelle was serving meals to homeless people who had come in that night. It was her first experience getting to know people who lived on the streets or in shelters, people who were part of the Toronto community. One dinner guest had a dog with him, so Michelle piled up a huge plate of turkey with gravy, potatoes, bread, and peas, and set the feast on the floor. The dog picked through the food and ate only the meat, leaving the rest. She assumed that the dog had been hungry and uncared for, but the plate of picked over food made a mess of her beliefs. How could someone who had no home take such good care of his animal? He wasn't doing a good job with his own life, she thought, but his dog was well fed and loved.

Michelle graduated that spring in 2001 and went off to New Zealand to practice for six months, but questions about homeless people and their pets remained. When she returned in 2003, she volunteered with the Ottawa Mission, an organization serving the homeless, and started treating clients' pets. Word spread that a veterinarian was treating the animals, and soon the doors of the Ottawa Mission's outreach clinics were swinging wider to allow people to come in with their pets.

While taking care of animals was Michelle's priority, it became clear that the dogs and cats were the entrée to reaching their owners. She'd been exposed to One Health concepts in school, and a stint in Kenya before veterinary college had shown her how important the health of herd animals is to the health of farmers, their families, and communities. Now in an urban setting, those lessons were becoming apparent in a new way. Treating someone's dog by vaccinating it against rabies or providing a wellness exam nurtured trust in the pet owner and opened a dialogue about his or her own well-being.

Michelle, a small Asian woman, says that her stature and gender make it easier for street youth to open up to her. She soon reached out to other social services beyond the Ottawa Mission. She lined up more agencies that worked with the homeless, convincing them to refer their animals for veterinary care with the hope that human health care would improve as well. She enlisted other veterinarians to volunteer with her. The more animals they saw, the more connections the social service staff could form with clients. They were getting a whole caseload of people from the vet outreach clinic. "One community health nurse said she had a youth who would never talk to her," Michelle remembers, "but when she told him she could get his dog into a community vet clinic, he started talking to her about a wound he [himself] had for months that wasn't healing."

After six years of volunteering part time while working full time as a veterinary associate and an animal behaviorist and teaching in a veterinary technician school, Michelle made a bigger move. In 2009, she formed the nonprofit Community Veterinary Outreach, putting together a board of directors of medical, veterinary, and social service people. She became CEO and with a team of volunteers started seeing animals through mobile units and at social service agencies.

Through Community Veterinary Outreach, Michelle witnessed the profound human-animal bond between homeless people and their animals, a bond that was different than the average devotion between mainstream pet owners and their animals. "My own research and other research shows that homeless people prioritize their animals over themselves," she says. "We understand that people who are marginalized and isolated—especially kids who often haven't grown up with adults who cared for them unconditionally—care very little for themselves. They've been abused, kicked out, or treated unfairly by adults, so they don't really have a sense of self-worth. Then they find an animal and experience humanity through the animal, and they'll do everything they can to take care of the animal. They actually learn to self-care and have worth through having a pet, which is remarkable to me."

The practice of treating pets and drawing their owners into self-care is a compelling example of One Health, but not everyone rushes to embrace the care of the homeless. Some people's compassion flows more easily toward animals than people. They have biases about homeless people and their pets, like the kind of biases Michelle had earlier in the church. However, after collecting data on thousands of animals over the last ten years, Michelle and her colleagues show that the animals are generally in good health, often in better health than their owners. The team used animal body condition scores and collected data on pet attachment scores, how long one has had a pet, where it was obtained, and whether one could afford care otherwise. Once people see that the animal is okay, then they can talk about the person. "Before then it's hard for people to focus on the roots of homelessness and how to solve societal issues," she says.

"For clients we leverage the human-animal bond to engage people in social services and health care," explains Michelle. "For the animals, we provide pro bono preventive veterinary care. For society, community, and social change, we leverage people's love of animals to talk about larger issues of homelessness, poverty, and economic disparity. We're able to go from there and ask why is it not okay for a dog to be on the street, but okay for a person to be on the street."

Since 2009, Community Veterinary Outreach model has been replicated, running five programs throughout Ontario. The impact has gone beyond pets and community health. Dozens of veterinary students volunteer at the clinics, developing their clinical skills and nurturing their understanding of this street-level One Health model.

Back in 2003, Michelle hadn't known what a social entrepreneur was. Now she's recognized as a leader, sharing her entrepreneurial skills. She's been able to compare the traditional corporate leadership programs with those that motivate and train social entrepreneurs, people who respond to societal inequities. During an internship at Ashoka, a global network of entrepreneurs, she discussed a "whole person leadership model" where leaders can demonstrate vulnerability and show it as strength. "In the corporate model, vulnerability means weakness and that you're not equipped to lead," she says. "But we see in veterinary medicine all the time that you can be upset and sad when you're euthanizing animals and still be viewed as a leader and as a professional. You can be professional and do your job and still have tears in your eyes."

This self-awareness has been a gift. As someone who failed college courses and was told she'd never get into vet school, Michelle fought hard to prove people wrong and to graduate veterinary college with distinction. But all that proving came from a place of fear: fear of failure. Now she says that her best leadership qualities come from vulnerability, and she takes on opportunities that allow her to explore strengths and weaknesses.

Today her goal is to help other people discover their own motivators to solve social problems, give them the confidence to put action to their ideas, and step back. She's currently working on a master's degree in social work, where she'll continue to explore health and wellness in a new direction. Like her fellow innovators, Michelle's peak moments are not tied to her own accomplishments. Instead, she thrives on helping people from all domains find their passion, work together, and make the world better for pets and their owners.

Justine puts in the sweat equity and urges all vets to apply for an LLC status so they can become business owners. Jane fills a huge gap in feline medicine and expands the profession as a leader through service. Michelle takes One Health to the street level through social entrepreneurism. Each of these women fuel their mission with passion, confidence, and hard work. Each of us can cultivate these qualities and follow their lead.

Takeaway Tips

- You don't have to be born with an entrepreneurial spirit to launch a business. Justine Lee has passion and vision, but she honed her skills by taking classes and putting sweat equity into her business ventures. The first easy step, she says, is to fill out the paperwork to become an LLC and start thinking of yourself as a business owner as soon as you become a veterinarian.
- Balance your business efforts with involvement in organized veterinary medicine. You can do well while doing good, and the connections and community you gain by serving through associations integrate your business and social sides, like Jane Brunt. However, pace yourself as you get involved, she advises. Like a computer, when you have too many windows open at a time, your operating system might crash.
- Follow your passions outside the clinic and volunteer in your community. Working on a volunteer basis can turn into a nonprofit business, as it did for Michelle Lem, and as a social entrepreneur you can make social change your business philosophy.

Notes

1.   Katty Kay and Claire Shipman, *The Confidence Code: The Art and Science of Self-Assurance—What Women Should Know* (New York: HarperBusiness, 2014).

2.   Helen Mills, "Can Entrepreneurship Be Taught?" *Canadian Woman Studies* 15, no. 1 (1994): 15–18.

3.   Veronica Collewaert and Frederik Anseel, "How Entrepreneurs Can Keep Their Passion From Fading," *Harvard Business Review*, June 16, 2016, https://hbr.org/2016/06/how-entrepreneurs-can-keep-their-passion-from-fading.

4.   Daniel McGinn, "Too Many Pivots, Too Little Passion," *Harvard Business Review*, September 2012, https://hbr.org/2012/09/too-many-pivots-too-little-passion.

5.   Jill Kickul and Norris Krueger, "Toward a New Model of Intentions: The Complexity of Gender, Cognitive Style, Culture, Social Norms, and Intensity on the Pathway to Entrepreneurship," Center for Gender in Organizations Simmons School of Management, http://www.simmons.edu/about-simmons/centers-organizations-and-institutes/cgo/publications/cgo-working-papers.

6.   Patrick Parker, "Change is Coming: What U.S. Colleges Must Do to Survive," *Wharton,* December 2, 2014, http://knowledge.wharton.upenn.edu/article/what-u-s-colleges-must-do-to-survive/.

7.   Kay and Shipman, *The Confidence Code.*

8.   "Social Entrepreneurship: Building the Field," *Ashoka Foundation,* https://www.ashoka.org/social_entrepreneur.

2

Leadership, Success, and the Happiness Quotient

I s she one? Are you one? Why don't they think they are? Who gets to be included into the women's leadership echelon and who doesn't? If we call some women leaders and others "just" managers, if we sanctify some as "visionary leaders" and others as mere directors, we risk placing the super achievers in the spotlight and relegating the other "average leaders" to the sidelines, missing out on the countless women with important lessons.

The idea of women's leadership is anything but one size fits all. Some leaders are the ones out front, in the corner office, or behind the microphone. Others are perfectly fine heading up teams, guiding from the sidelines or out of view. From the extraordinary to the everyday leader, veterinary medicine is a profession directed by more and more women. If they're making a positive impact on those around them and influencing the field, we consider them leaders and, more importantly, so do they.

"Veterinarians are leaders in their communities, and students need to think that way as soon as they graduate," says Eastern Region Assistant Director for Student Initiatives of the AVMA Dr. Anna Reddish. Dr. Tom Johnson agrees and adds that with leadership comes responsibility. In rural areas, says the director of hospital operations at Iowa State University (ISU), veterinarians are often the most highly educated in their towns and therefore have a responsibility to give back. "We introduce the idea of servant-leadership to ISU students and encourage it all the way through their involvement in the state association," he says.

"If leadership is influence, then all veterinarians are, to one extent or another, leaders, even if only in their own clinics," say Drs. Karen Bradley, Betsy Charles, and Joan Hendricks in the *Journal of the American Veterinary Medical Association* (*JAVMA*) article "A renewed call for veterinary leaders."[1] But, say the authors, influence at all levels, expanded and developed beyond individual patient care, is critical so that veterinarians lead and influence the profession for the greater good of society.

We agree with the basic definition that a leader is someone who directs, guides, or inspires others, but beyond that we're interested in broadening the discussion of women's leadership. Given all the factors that facilitate and hinder women's desire and capacity to lead, our goal is to create a more nuanced conversation that occurs at the juncture of leadership, success, and happiness—that sweet spot that changes over time for each woman. Depending on a slew of life issues like goals, age, motherhood, and money, the interplay of leadership, success, and happiness is as dynamic and individual as women themselves.

Why Are There Few Women at the Upper Echelons of Leadership?

Although the profession has more women than men, leadership in the major domains—practice, academia, industry, and organized veterinary medicine—is 70 to 80 percent male. Why do we have this large gender gap at top levels? The veterinary student population shifted to 50 percent women over 30 years ago and the general veterinary population shifted to over 50 percent in 2007, so why do levels of women's leadership hover at 20 to 30 percent? The answers are anything but simple.

According to Bradley, Charles, and Hendricks, veterinarians (male and female), much like their counterparts in human medicine, are trained as individual healers whose greatest impact is on hands-on patient care. "Both tend to be comfortable in practice environments and do not necessarily look for opportunities to have a voice in the larger issues facing society," they say.[2] Exceptions abound, as demonstrated by robust student leadership groups and the 20 to 30 percent of women leaders at top levels across the profession. Nevertheless, many argue that the majority of students who excel in sciences and pursue veterinary medicine are more inclined toward animal science and less inclined toward influence for the sake of social change. "A lot of us identify more as scientists and doctors than political and social change types," said one student at a recent Student American Veterinary Medical Association (SAVMA) symposium.

Still, for women who *do* want to become leaders outside the clinical environment, career and life experiences are different than those of their male colleagues. These women face countless factors that influence their leadership paths—so many that it's easy to imagine the woman who does reach an upper echelon as an archetype, the kind who plows through all the outside forces, head down and single-minded, until she reaches her career goal. Perhaps the typical female veterinary leader looks more like a woman dancing, weaving a career path through the challenges and delights of caring for others, extra demands on time, and, often, motherhood.

The myriad factors that influence women's veterinary leadership seems to fall into two broad categories: personal choice and external pressure. Deciding to live in one's home state where plum veterinary jobs are scarce is a personal choice. Pursuing independent research instead of becoming head of a lab is a personal choice. Working in a clinic as an associate rather than buying a practice is a personal choice. Finding a job with a flexible schedule in order to be home with children *might be* a personal choice, or it might be a result of lack of affordable child care (more on that later).

Then there are choices stemming from realities that impinge on opportunities: motherhood and the extra work it creates at home; limitations in family leave policies and programs; and salary differences. It is essential to our understanding of leadership, success, and happiness that we appreciate the different kinds of women's choices: choices they make for their individual goals and interests, and the choices they *have to* make from external realities that, frankly, affect women differently than men.

Along with choices unique to women comes a set of obstacles that, again, are theirs alone. Some stem from women's internal, psychological obstacles—what Dr. Carla Oleska, gender specialist and motivational speaker, calls the glass ceiling within.[3] Examples of these kind of obstacles include perfectionism, feeling like an impostor, self-doubt, and avoiding conflict. These internal barriers are discussed in this book's chapter "Beyond Fake It 'Til You Make It." The external obstacles that women regularly hurdle come from subtle yet persistent cultural influences and gender stereotypes, along with organizational practices that are biased toward men. None is insurmountable but taken together, these small and larger obstacles add up to significant challenges. Some assert that the glass ceiling has been shattered and what remains is a concrete wall to climb. Psychology professors Alice Eagly and Linda Carli describe a serpentine path to leadership in their book *Through the Labyrinth*, discussing the multiple factors from responsibilities at home to inflexible workplaces that contribute to the shortage of women leaders.[4] Whether a labyrinth, leaky pipeline, concrete wall, or glass ceiling, the metaphors convey a common truth: women face more challenges than men when they aim for top positions.

There are several important explorations of gender differences and how they affect leadership choices and obstacles in veterinary medicine, notably *JAVMA* contributions like the article by Bradley, Charles, and Hendricks, as well as "Women in Veterinary Medicine," by Margaret and Miriam Slater,[5] "Gender and Work: What Veterinarians Can Learn from Research about Women, Men and Work," by Carin Smith,[6] and "Future Needs and Recommendations for Leadership in Veterinary Medicine," by James W. Lloyd, Lonnie J. King, Carol A. Mase, and Donna Harris.[7] In "Gender Work in a Feminized Profession: The Case of Veterinary Medicine," authors Leslie Irvine and Jenny R. Vermilya argue that veterinary medicine, despite being numerically dominated by women, is "gendered masculine" and that its culture "values masculine characteristics, such as the freedom from familial responsibility."[8] Each offers insight; however, a full examination and data-driven analysis of the multiple issues facing women's leadership is still needed in the field. That examination is beyond the scope of this book. Instead, we explore some of the big choices and obstacles, and throughout the ensuing chapters we profile women who have become leaders while integrating their choices and addressing the challenges.

Personal Choices, Relationships, and the Long and Winding Career Path

Women today have more opportunities than in the past, but they also have more choices to integrate into their lives and careers than men do. Through our research and interviews, most women readily acknowledge the role of parenting and partner relationships in their careers or, if they're single or do not have children, in the careers of their colleagues. Others minimize mention of kids, parents, and significant others because they want to be viewed as "purely professionals," a term that assumes that professionals of either gender don't integrate their insights or sensitivities as parents or partners into their work as doctors who work with animals and clients.

Amanda Bisol, University of Pennsylvania VMD 2011, bought a practice one and a half years out of veterinary school and recently had her third child, and she's proud that her personal and professional life rarely mix in public. "Very few of my clients even know I'm a mother," she says. Others routinely reveal their motherhood, like Dr. Linda Jacobson, practice owner in New York City and 1971 Tuskegee University DVM, who even once placed her infant in the arms of a grieving client to help ease the pain of having to euthanize his dog.

While it's up to them to decide, more and more women today, because of shifting attitudes and practices, feel comfortable exposing their multiple sides in the workplace, especially in a caring domain like veterinary practice. Now that women are the norm in the profession, their expertise as doctors is less likely to be scrutinized if they reveal that they're also mothers and caretakers. "[Women] agree that professional achievement should be based on objective standards of training and performance," Margaret R. Slater and Miriam Slater note in the *JAVMA* article "Women in Veterinary Medicine."[9] The authors add that female veterinarians are committed to merit standards while acknowledging differing needs at specific times in the life cycle for women, as well as for men. Irvine and Vermilya argue that being compassionate is a quality that women use to define themselves, but that when they run their practices many strive to interact in a more masculine way and charge more for their services.[10]

Motherhood is the ultimate relationship, but relationships in general are an essential characteristic of women's lives. Being relational is one of women's identifying qualities, and it shapes the choices they make about success and leadership. Making others a priority doesn't mean that they're unambitious or uninterested in powerful, high-level careers. Nor does it mean that they're falling back into traditional, sexist roles of the past if they weave other interests and goals into their lives beyond work. "Women define themselves by more than their work," Lisa Mainiero and Sherry Sullivan mention in *The Opt Out Revolt: Why People Are Leaving Companies to Create Kaleidoscope Careers.*[11] "The focus on relationships isn't a shortcoming of women's lives," they say, "but a feature of their career development and choices."

If women decide to take time off from their original career plan to raise children full or part time, it doesn't mean they don't care as much about their careers as men or other women. It just means that the norm for women is to make space and take time for children, parents, extended family, spouses, and friends—all while doing the best they can at work. This isn't to say that men don't value their relationships or wouldn't take a more circuitous career path if that were encouraged. Men, too, nurture their relationships, but when they break stereotypes and become a primary or even partial caretaker, they're viewed as the anomaly. Sometimes they're supported by their peers, but more often than not they're viewed askance, and besides, like women, they have very limited workplace flexibility. Paternity leave, while available in many places, isn't widely utilized in the United States, and it is very rarely incentivized as it is in some European countries.[12]

Whether backed by neuroscience or reinforced by culture, relationships and connectedness feature prominently in women's careers.[13] The rub is that it's faster to get to the top when the trajectory is single-focused and uninterrupted, and women's trajectories are wider and more winding in order to fold in multiple goals and people into their lives.

Gender Stereotypes and Leadership

Conventional beliefs hold that women's leadership styles are more partic-ipatory and collaborative than those of their male counterparts, and that they're more empathetic and supportive in the workplace. That belief is consistent with how women talk about themselves and how our culture expects them to act; however, most research shows no gender difference in evaluations of leaders by supervisors, subordinates, and peers in real-world settings.[14] So why the disconnect between what people believe and what studies reveal?

"Gender stereotypes and cultural expectations shape women to behave and describe their own behavior in ways that are consistent with conven-tional notions of femininity,"[15] Barbara Kellerman and Deborah Rhode note in *Women and Leadership: The State of Play and Strategies for Change*. "Today, leadership and management practices call for both sexes to be more collaborative and interpersonally savvy." In other words, women and men who work collaboratively, who nurture their teams, and who have honed their communication skills will be more successful, regardless of whether these qualities are innately female.

Do women leaders empower others and lead through cooperative, collaborative approaches more so than men? Are women more nurturing? These are the wrong questions. Better to ask how can we celebrate men and women who lead in ways that bring out the best qualities in their teams, who are looked up to as people who know when to use different styles—directive, collaborative, inspirational, or plainspoken—in order to achieve goals that serve a greater good. When there are differences in approach, we shouldn't ask which is better or who is a leader or a follower, a man or a woman. We should ask which leadership approach is most effective in bringing out the best in others, getting the job done, and advancing the profession.

So what's the right way?

Some rely on jurisdictional power alone—that is, power that comes from their title or post. Helen S. Astin and Carole Leland describe in *Women of Influence, Women of Vision* the difference between command and leadership. The former comes from your office, and anyone who has the office can command.[16] Leaders in today's world need to have extraordinary self-awareness and very strong interpersonal and communication skills. They need to know their strengths and qualities, and play to these strengths, rather than trying to be all things to all people. They need to be confident enough to surround themselves with strong, outspoken, brilliant people. They need to be excellent listeners, and know how to build agreement, to network, to bring people together and to inspire them to work hard for a shared vision.

Motherhood and Leadership

"Women can have it all but probably not all at once," says Dr. Jacobson, the veterinarian who helped the grieving client. The only barrier to women's leadership now, she says, is that woman bear children, and their biological needs before, during, and after childbirth make it hard to achieve the imagined, seamless fusion of leadership and motherhood.

If "having it all" is a goal of the new generation of leaders, then they have to figure out finances, timing of childbirth, and division of labor at home. Actually, it's not just *they* but *we*, all of us in the profession, who have to figure it out together. We can all help younger women see their lives as journeys, easing the stress of having to accomplish everything by a certain age.[17] Anne-Marie Slaughter's 2012 *Atlantic* article "Why Women Still Can't Have It All, Or Can They?"[18] was one of the most read and commented on articles in the history of the magazine. Language shapes ideas, and for Slaughter, "work/life fit" is preferable than "work/life balance" or "juggling career and home." Her plea is that women and men come together to "change how we think, how we talk, how we plan and work and vote."[19]

Careers, Double Duty at Home, and Happiness

Work-life balance, work-life fit, integration, equilibrium—whatever one calls it, working life is more challenging than ever because the work side of the equation keeps increasing. The blessings of the digital age— being able to work from home, checking emails on the go, getting back to clients quickly—come with the dark side. Always being on call, after work requests from clients about their pets, and never unplugging are just a few. The forty-hour workweek has gone the way of the horse-drawn carriage. Researchers at the Cornell Employment and Family Careers Institute show that the combined workweek of dual earner couples has increased by ten hours a week for salaried workers. Couples where one or more of the partners are professionals are half to 90 percent more likely to feel overworked than in the past. Single parents are not only overworked but, not surprisingly, enjoy less free time.[20]

What women do at home and what men do at home affects the equation when women strive for work-life balance. For those who take time off to raise children, the costs are both obvious and hidden. For college-educated women, the calculation over their lifetimes is upward of a million dollars for this "mommy tax." Women pay the price whether they're mothers or not because they usually assume the caregiver role and are also responsible for older relatives. And as our elders live longer, the caretaking role stretches longer into women's lives. In other words, it starts early with young children and extends far into later years with elders. While caretaking can be a joy, it does come with an economic cost. The cost in lost wages, Social Security benefits, and pensions over their lifetimes is extremely high, and considering that most women live longer than their male partners, the significance is huge.[21] The economy of care, as MacArthur Genius Awardee and economist Nancy Folbre[22] describes, depends on women but doesn't compensate them.

Veterinarians train to be professionals, and like many professionals, they have expectations of egalitarian relationships. While few studies have been done among veterinarians, a recent study of Harvard Business School graduates reveals that the vast majority of female graduates initially expect their career and their spouse's career to rank equally. However, among those who have children, more than two-thirds end up doing most of the child care.[23] Before the Harvard alumnae had children, there was no gender gap—men and women each did about 14.5 hours of housework a week. But after a birth, women's total work—including paid work, housework, and child care—increased an additional 21 hours a week while men's increased just 12.5 hours. For women, but not men, child care did not substitute for any of their existing work; it was all supplemental.[24] Attitudes in the general professional population inform how veterinarians might be thinking about and struggling with work and family expectations.

The elusive quest for balance, if there really is such a thing, is fraught with economic decisions—when can I go back to work full or part time; should one of us work part time; can we afford day care; can we afford elder care for grandma? Because women bear children and end up doing more at home, the decisions are fueled by a hefty dose of exhaustion and emotion. Most women talk about a feeling of perpetual guilt. They're either guilt-ridden for not being at home if they work full time, or at every single game if they work part time, or for buying the cookies instead of baking them. Or they feel guilty for not staying late at work, not arriving early, not emailing a client within five hours, or not going to that veterinary conference.

Most workplaces offer inadequate family benefits, and practices, most particularly small practices, are challenged by hiring, training, and ultimately offering flexible hours to veterinarians who choose to raise children. It leaves working parents with a terrible choice between career and family, advancement and stasis, challenge at work and changing diapers at home, full income and saving resources, and on and on. The opt-out phenomenon is the upshot for some, and it takes a variety of forms, according to authors Mainiero and Sullivan. Some women leave the workforce for good while others work part time or return full time when their children are older. Some launch their own businesses from home.

Sometimes the harshest critics of women's choices are other women. One student recalled a conversation with a prominent female equine practitioner, a seasoned owner who years earlier broke into the ranks of a predominantly male field. Describing "today's generation of younger women," the senior veterinarian criticized women who wanted to take time off for their families, who didn't want to put in the hard work that she herself did. This comment is based on the sentiment that "I worked hard, dealt with discrimination, and sacrificed other goals, so you should, too." Generational differences along with gender play a very big part in pathways to the top, and combined with the tough attitudes and moxie that were essential to the success of many of the trailblazers, we need even greater communication and understanding for progress.

Changing behaviors at home is a great way to start, and changing them in the workplace and legislatures is vitally important, but changing them among women themselves would go a long way to supporting all women's choices. Many women say that the demands from employers, clients, spouses, and inadequate family leave policies are compounded when they feel critiqued for their choices by other women. Stay-at-home mothers, women who work full time, part time, or overtime all can cheer each other on since everyone seems to be dancing as fast as they can.

Workplaces

While some workplaces aren't family-friendly, many are trying to be. Veterinary practices are often small or sole proprietaries and struggle to offer flexible scheduling. But being small doesn't have to be the death knell for a practice that wants to attract and retain top talent. The Onion River Animal Hospital in Montpelier, Vermont, for example, is owned by three women. As co-owners, they come up with a schedule that supports each of their needs and schedules. Dr. Colleen Bloom, who started the practice when she was a single mother with an infant son, is now a co-owner and is content working part time so she can travel and spend time with her son, now grown with his own family, and enjoy her grandchildren. Very active in her state association, including having served as its president, she models women's leadership by creating flexibility with her co-owners.

Dr. Karen Bradley, another co-owner, works a modified schedule in order to be active in the lives of her two children. Bradley also takes on leadership roles at the AVMA, including former chair and vice chair of the House Advisory Committee, and was elected in 2016 to the prestigious Board of Directors when there were just three voting women on the fifteen-person board. As cofounder of the Women's Veterinary Leadership Development Initiative (WVLDI), she is dedicated to promoting women's leadership and encouraging other women to get involved in organized veterinary medicine and consider becoming owners of a practice. Responding to women practice associates who are apprehensive about owning a practice because of fear of more responsibilities and lack of freedom, the third

Onion River co-owner, Dr. Lauren Quinn, says that the co-owner model turns the independence concern "on its head," because she makes decisions about the practice, its finances, and her time off, all the while building equity in a practice she owns. One trap that sensitive practices like Onion River avoid is making sure that the childless veterinarian isn't routinely "volunteered" for covering for family-centered holidays, a complaint that some in the field have voiced.

Money

Everyone in veterinary medicine knows that the return on investment of a DVM education hasn't kept pace with the skyrocketing cost of the education. The national mean of a veterinary education in 2015 was more than $150,000, over twice what it was fifteen years earlier, according to the 2015 AVMA "Report on the Market for Veterinarians."[25] Swirling around these numbers are vigorous debates about the increasing spread between debt and starting salaries, which is now well over twice the mean starting salary of a new graduate, the perceived oversupply of veterinarians, the emergence of new United States veterinary colleges, the increase in class size of many existing colleges, and the accreditation of foreign veterinary schools. Students know that their medical counterparts, physicians, make significantly more as a starting salary (post-residency) and that there's actually a cry for more general practitioners in the medical field.

What many students don't know, however, is that salaries between male and female veterinarians differ greatly in some fields, but especially in private practice, where men make over 30 percent more than women, without accounting for any variables from hours worked to type of practice to role in the practice. As data are teased apart, students face startling results that only recently are becoming clearer. For example, there is a marked difference in compensation between practice owners and associates, with women associates yielding a mere 2 percent return on estimated average return for obtaining a DVM considering the total cost of education, according to the 2011 "Workforce Needs in Veterinary Medicine."[26] Another finding is that women practice owners in some fields receive over 40 percent less compensation than their male counterparts while often working comparable hours. As students become aware of this and other stark facts, they often react differently to the challenges of becoming a leader, focusing instead on the more immediate concern for getting a greater return from their educational expenditures.

In our sessions with students and early career practitioners, we preside over vigorous discussions about why women owners receive lower compensation than men for their veterinary services. Are they working more in general practices where salaries are less than in specialty practices? Do they charge less for their service, or perform more pro bono work? Are they sharing more of their income with staff, or reinvesting more back into their practices? At this point there are no comprehensive studies examining these questions. The AVMA economics division, for its part, continues to study the issue, reflecting a commitment of the association to have better answers and solutions to the gender pay gap. Irvine and Vermilya argue that "economic success often required dis-identifying with the feminine."[27] The authors' study sample size was small but all said they did not doubt women's abilities to own a successful practice. However, some said that "being a woman led to ineffective business practices." In general, Irvine and Vermilya found that female veterinarians don't charge enough for their services "because they have more compassion for the client than the man would."[28]

One thing that has remained consistent in recent years is that there is less gender variability in starting salaries for men and women than there is later in their careers. For example, the difference between starting male and female salaries for new graduates in companion animal practice varies by between 1 and 4 percent—men higher—while the variation for those entering mixed animal practice is closer to 10 percent. Though the impact of these starting differences may compound over time and result in a greater income disparity, other variables such as difference metrics for compensation besides salary also need to be considered.

Even though many veterinarians hiring new associates assure us that they make no salary distinction on the basis of gender, it is well known that women in general are more reluctant to negotiate than their male classmates, a behavior apparent in other fields beyond veterinary medicine. Books and seminars on negotiation only reach veterinary students in dribbles, sometimes through an elective workshop offered by business clubs to the students already oriented toward those offerings, or through a one-credit class on professionalism crammed into the third year right before starting clinical rotations.

Without awareness and relevant skill-building, female veterinarians will likely adopt the same limiting attitudes and behaviors that befall other women. Across disciplines, women are two and a half times more likely than men to feel "a great deal of apprehension" about negotiating, and men are about four times more likely to initiate negotiations. When asked to pick metaphors for the negotiating process, men picked "winning a ballgame" and a "wrestling match," while women picked "going to the dentist." Twenty percent of adult women (22 million people) say they never negotiate at all, even though they often recognize negotiation as appropriate and even necessary.[29] Women often don't know the market value of their work. They report salary expectations between 3 and 32 percent lower than those of men for the same jobs; men expect to earn 13 percent more than women during their first year of full-time work and 32 percent more at their career peaks. According to one study, by not negotiating a first salary, an individual stands to lose more than $500,000 by age sixty.[30]

In the competitive job environment, many female veterinarians are so grateful just to receive a job offer or one that will offer flexibility for family considerations that they don't even consider negotiating for a higher starting salary, whereas men approach the situation differently. Clearly they can improve their negotiating skills when they're starting out and as they move up. Male employers, whether in veterinary medicine or elsewhere, may become defensive when faced with the gender compensation differences because they feel they are being unfairly targeted for paying women less when, in fact, the causes are multiple and relate to differences in behaviors and structural impediments that may have nothing to do with trying to constrain women's compensation.

Some states are working toward gender pay parity legislatively. Massachusetts recently became the first state to bar employers from asking applicants about their salaries before offering them a job. Still, negotiation experts Linda Babcock and Sara Laschever say that organizations can do a lot to address the negotiation differences between male and female employees. Managers can mentor women in their organizations about the importance of letting their supervisors know what they want and what would help them do their jobs better.[31] Employers can change their mindsets, trying to bring out the best for both parties rather than just considering the bottom lines of their payrolls. Putting business goals on the table, employers should invite their female candidate to propose numbers—salary, time, and benefits—that work for both. Why? Not as altruistic acts of gender equality, though applauded, but because it's good for business and for the profession.

"If you want someone to do their best for your clinic, they need to know how much you value them," writes Ryan Gates, DVM. "When it comes to hiring a new associate, whether a potential business partner or a short-term part-timer, your salary offer is your first chance to express that value—and you know what they say about first impressions."[32] Gates doesn't merely understand gender differences; he works with them. "Women generally don't negotiate like men. Expecting them to do so is unrealistic, and deliberately using the knowledge that they don't is unethical," he says. "One reason women don't negotiate like men is that they can get worse outcomes when they negotiate than when they don't."[33]

Gates says that because a largely female pool of potential replacements is poised to step into employment and ownership positions currently held by men, it's crucial that we account for gender differences in negotiating, employing, and working in order to secure a financially healthy profession for us all. "This means being aware of gender preferences in salary negotiation," he says, "and interpreting the other person's actions and responses based on a common frame of reference—not just our own."[34]

Is Confidence a Factor in the Wage Gap?

AVMA economist Dr. Mike Dicks and his team wanted to examine whether confidence was at the root of the gender wage gap in the general population, and if it applied to the gap between male and female veterinarians.[35] Does confidence play a role in both the wage gap and in job performance? Previous research has shown that women tend to demonstrate less confidence and less competitiveness than men. On the other hand, if a job is female-oriented, men show less confidence than women.

Dicks's team used data from the 2015 AVMA Employment Survey[36] sent to every veterinarian who graduated one and five years previously. In 2014, according to the survey, the national mean annual earnings for these veterinarians was $74,253. Women had mean annual earnings of $71,714, while men had mean annual earnings of $83,538, a wage gap of 16.5 percent.

Aside from gender, factors contributing to the wage gap include: graduation year, age, board certification, additional degrees held, whether the respondent served an internship, practice type, hours worked per week, and region. Controlling for all these factors, the study showed that the gender wage gap was just over 8.5 percent, still quite significant and, it turns out, perplexing. The researchers asked both male and female survey respondents to rate their levels of clinical competencies in twelve areas, ranging from physical examinations to anesthesia to fluid therapy. Women rated themselves higher than men on all areas, ruling out confidence as a reason for the wage gap, according to the economics team. But there very well may be a disconnect between how women rate their competence on surveys and how they demonstrate their confidence in negotiating salary and charging clients.

The wage gap isn't as much as a mystery to solve as a puzzle with many pieces. Differences in negotiation is one puzzle piece. Women's tendency to undercharge clients is another. Women paying employees higher rates is a third. The difference between males and females in specialty practices versus general practice is yet another piece. In all its complexity, the salary gap is essential to close but is only one part of the leadership gap.

Winding career paths, gender stereotypes, psychological barriers, motherhood, double duty at home, salary gap—the obstacles seem dizzying. And yet women calibrate their demands each day and carve their paths to success and happiness. Those who go on to become leaders despite the array of challenges are especially remarkable. Their stories shine as examples of optimism and determination. Shared in the following pages, they illuminate a wider path for all of us.

Notes

1.　Karen Bradley, Betsy Charles, and Joan Hendricks, "A Renewed Call for Veterinary Leaders," *Journal of the American Veterinary Medical Association* 247, no. 6 (2015): 592–94, https://doi.org/10.2460/javma.247.6.592.

2.　Ibid.

3.　Dr. Carla Oleska, in discussion with the authors, 2014.

4.　Alice H. Eagly and Linda L. Carli, *Through the Labyrinth: The Truth About How Women Become Leaders* (Boston: Harvard Business School Press, 2007).

5.　Margaret R. Slater and Miriam Slater, "Women in Veterinary Medicine," *Journal of the American Veterinary Medical Association* 217, no. 4 (2000): 273–76, https://doi.org/10.2460/javma.2000.217.472.

6.　Carin Smith, "Gender and Work: What Veterinarians Can Learn from Research About Women, Men, and Work," *Journal of the American Veterinary Medical Association* 220, no. 9 (2002): 1304–11, https://doi.org/10.2460/javma.2002.220.1304.

7.　James W. Lloyd, Lonnie J. King, Carol A. Mase, and Donna Harris, "Future Needs and Recommendations for Leadership in Veterinary Medicine," *Journal of the American Veterinary Medical Association* 226, no. 7 (2005): 1060–67. http://dx.doi.org/10.2460/javma.2005.226.1060.

8.　Leslie Irvine and Jenny R. Vermilya, "Gender Work in a Feminized Profession: The Case of Veterinary Medicine," *Gender and Society* 24, no. 1 (2010): 56–82, http://dx.doi.org/10.1177/0891243209355978.

9.　Slater and Slater, "Women in Veterinary Medicine," 274.

10.　Irvine and Vermilya, "Gender Work in a Feminized Profession," 56.

11.　Lisa Mainiero and Sherry Sullivan, *The Opt-Out Revolt: Why People Are Leaving Companies to Start Kaleidoscope Careers* (Boston: Nicholas Brealey America, 2006).

12.　Ariel Meysam Ayanna, "Aggressive Parental Leave Incentivizing: A Statutory Proposal Toward Gender Equalization in the Workplace," *University of Pennsylvania Journal of Business Law* 293 (2007): 293–324, http://scholarship.law.upenn.edu/jbl/vol9/iss2/2.

13.　Joan V. Gallos, "Exploring Women's Development: Implications for Career, Theory, Practice and Research," in *Handbook of Career Theory*, ed. Michael B. Arthur, Douglas T. Hall, and Barbara S. Lawrence (New York: Cambridge

University Press, 1996), 110–32; Dianna Hales, *Just Like a Woman: How Gender Science is Redefining What Makes Us Female* (New York: Bantam, 1999); Judith M. Bardwick, "The Seasons of a Women's Life," in *Women's Lives: New Theory, Research and Policy*, ed. Dorothy G. McGuigan (Ann Arbor: University of Michigan, 1980), 35–37.

14.   Barbara Kellerman and Deborah L. Rhode, *Women and Leadership: The State of Play and Strategies for Change* (San Francisco: Wiley and Sons, 2007).

15.   Ibid, 7.

16.   Helen S. Astin and Carole Leland, *Women of Influence, Women of Vision: A Cross-Generational Study of Leaders and Social Change* (San Francisco: Jossey-Bass, 1991).

17.   Sheryl Sandberg, *Lean In: Women, Work and the Will to Lead* (New York: Knopf, 2013).

18.   Anne-Marie Slaughter, "Why Women Still Can't Have It All," *Atlantic*, July 2012, http://www.theatlantic.com/magazine/archive/2012/07/why-women -still-cant-have-it-all/309020/.

19.   Jonathon A. Knee, "Closing the Gender Gap by Changing Minds," *New York Times*, October 2, 2015, http://www.nytimes.com/2015/10/03/business /dealbook/unfinished-business-review-closing-gender-gap.html?_r=0.

20.   Bickley Townsend, "Dissecting the Time Squeeze," *Cornell Employment and Family Careers Institute, Bronfenbrenner Life Course Center Issue Briefs* 3, no. 1 (2002): 1–4.

21.   Ann Crittenden, *The Price of Motherhood* (New York: Henry Holt and Company, 2001); Economic Mobility Pathways, "Massachusetts Economic Independence Index," http://s3.amazonaws.com/empath-website/pdf/Research -MAEconomicIndependenceIndex-0313.pdf.

22.   Nancy Folbre, *The Invisible Heart: Economics and Family Values* (New York: New Press, 2001).

23.   Alison Wood Brooks and Francesca Gino, "Explaining Gender Differences at the Top," *Harvard Business Review*, September 23, 2015, https:// hbr.org/2015/09/explaining-gender-differences-at-the-top.

24.   Claire Cane Miller, "Men Do More at Home, But Not as Much as They Think," *New York Times*, November 12, 2015, http://www.nytimes .com/2015/11/12/upshot/men-do-more-at-home-but-not-as-much-as-they-think -they-do.html?_r=0.

25.   Michael R. Dicks, Ross Knippenberg, Bridgette Bain, and Lisa Greenhill, *2015 AVMA Report on the Market for Veterinary Education,* October 2015, http://dx.doi.org/10.13140/RG.2.1.3797.8003.

26.   National Research Council, *Workforce Needs in Veterinary Medicine* (Washington, DC: National Academies Press, 2011).

27.   Leslie Irvine and Jenny R. Vermilya, "Gender Work in a Feminized Profession: The Case of Veterinary Medicine," *Gender and Society* 24, no. 1 (2010): 73, http://dx.doi.org/10.1177/0891243209355978.

28.   Ibid, 72.

29.   Linda Babcock and Sara Laschever, *Women Don't Ask: The High Cost of Avoiding Negotiation—and Positive Strategies for Change* (New York: Princeton University Press, 2003).

30.   Linda Babcock and Sara Laschever, "Women Don't Ask: Negotiation and the Gender Divide," http://www.womendontask.com/stats.html.

31.   Ibid.

32.   Ryan Gates, "How to Figure Out What to Pay an Associate Veterinarian: Don't Skimp—You Want This Asset to Feel Valued," *DVM360,* October 1, 2014, http://veterinarybusiness.dvm360.com/figuring-out-what-pay-associate -veterinarian.

33.   Ibid.

34.   Ibid.

35.   Yaoqin Shen, Ross Knippenberg, and Mike Dicks, "The Gender Wage Gap in Veterinary Medicine: Is Clinical Confidence a Factor?" *DVM360,* October 1, 2015, http://veterinarynews.dvm360.com/gender-wage-gap-veterinary -medicine-clinical-confidence-factor.

36.   Michael R. Dicks, Ross Knippenberg, Bridgette Bain, and Lisa Greenhill, *2015 AVMA Report on the Market for Veterinary Education,* October 2015, http://dx.doi.org/10.13140/RG.2.1.3797.8003.

3

Doggedness

From literature to proverb, from pop psychology to parents' wisdom, the world is full of messages about overcoming adversity. What doesn't kill you makes you stronger. When the going gets tough, the tough get going. Business gurus, basketball greats, preachers, and grandmothers all tell us in their inimitable way how hardship is the stuff of life and how we handle the hardship is the stuff that builds character. Maya Angelou is among the most eloquent, saying, "We many encounter many defeats, but we must not be defeated. In fact, it may be necessary to encounter the defeats so you can know who you are, what you can rise from, how you can still come out of it."[1]

With an average acceptance rate of 50 percent at veterinary colleges,[2] the road to a veterinary education, graduation, and that first job requires more than your average "follow your dream" focus. For top academic achievers, it takes an ability to deal with less than perfect grades once they get to school and a terrier-like determination to forge their careers after they graduate. For people who faced extra obstacles along the way, their achievements gleam especially bright.

The women in this chapter faced challenges that were different than the usual struggles—poor grades, difficult situations at home, crushing debt—and their backgrounds set them apart from the average students of their time. Many were trailblazers: the first in her family to go to college, one of the first women of color in a student body of nearly all white men, one of the first white women at an historically black school, the first female practice owner in her area, or the first female president

45

of her state association. The very doggedness that got these women through the doors of their veterinary colleges shaped them into the leaders they ultimately became.

Some people get worn down by their challenges, even when rising to heights of leadership. Stress, fatigue, health issues, or bitterness erode their achievements, sometimes as background problems that hum distractingly or, worse, as serious issues that dominate their lives. Rare are the leaders who are willing to reveal their dark side; those stories usually aren't displayed as pictures of success. Yet the full picture—the easy and the ugly—are candid tales of how people lead in spite of their obstacles. The stories here highlight the stressors as well as the triumphs in veterinary medicine. For a profession with a relatively high rate of depression and suicide, we hope to help veterinarians thrive emotionally and professionally.

Along with the leaders who struggle with the residue of earlier challenges are others who seem to become stronger, even graceful, because of their challenges. Some seem blessed with innate positivity, embodying optimism and wisdom during the throes of difficulties, and some draw on the strength of family, friends, or faith. Of course, most people slide between negativity and positivity throughout the arc of their lives. Dr. Linda Jacobson had a dear friend, a black woman, who helped her stay positive during her time at Tuskegee as one of the first white female students. Dr. Sylvia Berg Salk was a trailblazer as one of the first women admitted to veterinary college in the early 1940s. Dr. Rachel Cezar used a health challenge to bring balance and wellness into her career. Dr. Ruby Perry's mother, active in the civil rights movement, was her lasting inspiration. Dr. Lila Miller's mentor, a West Indian man practicing in Harlem, helped her heal her bitterness of experiencing racism and reminded her time and again to "let it go."

Along with a strong support system, a common thread among these leaders is their willingness, perhaps their need, to give back. So strong is the desire to make things better for others that their very professionalism becomes infused with servitude and volunteerism Dr. Jacobson became president of her alumni association and her state association. Dr. Salk bridged human and animal health here and abroad long before One Health was coined. Dr. Cezar volunteers in a pre-vet program for first-generation college students at her alma mater. Dr. Perry became dean of Tuskegee's veterinary college where she earned her degree. Dr. Miller served on the New York State Board of Veterinary Medicine, a group she had originally shunned.

The veterinary leaders who have dealt with significant challenges inspire us in profound ways. They teach us that tenacity paired with optimism and generosity makes remarkable people. They show us that, like so many adages say, strength is a product of adversity. Rather than simply admire them, they inspire us to cultivate our own inner strength, optimism, and resiliency.

More than that, however, is a lesson for those in positions of power: in admissions, on hiring committees, or on faculty and board recruitment committees. The lesson is to open the gates a little wider to allow in people who don't fit the traditional mold of student, practitioner, faculty member, or volunteer. We applaud gatekeepers who actively seek nontraditional individuals and take a chance on people who might not have the full package of skills up front. That boldness will result in a more dynamic, interesting student body or workforce, and it will quite possibly result in an extraordinary leader. The veterinary profession and society will be strengthened when we recruit, include, and champion the broadest possible type of veterinarian. It's not an act of charity to encourage diversity, but an act of change.

Dr. Linda Jacobson

A young, white woman drove down from Brooklyn to Alabama's Tuskegee Institute (now University), enrolling as the second white woman at the historically black veterinary college. It was 1967, and Alabama sat directly on the fault lines of racial shifts that were rocking the South and the nation. Linda Jacobson had left behind the coffee shops and folk scene of Greenwich Village to pursue her dream of becoming a veterinarian, leaving the counterculture of the North and entering the civil rights upheavals in the South. The march on Selma took place just before she arrived in Alabama, and she remembers the protests that erupted one year later when Martin Luther King Jr. was assassinated. "Students were marching with two-by-fours up to the vet school. I understood the rage but didn't want to be a victim of it," said Linda. On that protest day, she drove the long way home instead of through the neighborhoods that might have been in upheaval.

Leadership sometimes involves overcoming substantial obstacles such as gender and race, and Linda, while slight and soft-spoken, is a poster girl for that kind of resoluteness. In a career that took her from Brooklyn to Alabama and from private practice to the presidency of the New York State association, her story might seem to be defined by gender and the era in which she went to school. A closer look, however, reveals that Linda's brand of leadership is less defined by her gender and experiences as a white woman in the South as it is a person whose determination got her there in the first place.

Resented alike by white store owners for going to a black school and by some black students for seemingly taking the place of black students, Linda was left wondering how she got into Tuskegee. She felt like she was being torn apart, she says. A few good friends helped her feel whole, and she remembers a particular outing, driving with her classmate from Tuskegee to Auburn, two friends black and white, and stopping at a truck stop to enjoy a nice meal. "We would have trucks following us with a gun rack in the back," she remembers. "Maybe that was just the 'we are never going to die mentality' of twenty-year-olds, but still—we were lucky to be alive in that time."

As life-changing as it was to be one of the first white female students at Tuskegee, Linda was deeply aware of the challenges of her black friends. Before the term *white privilege* gained awareness, she knows that her experiences were very different than what her Tuskegee friends faced every day. What united them in some ways were the challenges of being accepted to veterinary college as women. For Linda, the road to vet school had been long and hard. Again, history played a role and the times, sang Greenwich Village icon Bob Dylan, they were a-changin'.

"I was applying to vet school at a time when women were not considered desirable students," says Linda. Criteria were totally different than today when it would be illegal to take only two women or to say "no city women." "My grades were not that great either," she says. "The world was expanding and New York City was expanding to me at that time. It was the 1960s and the city was the best place in the world to be. I was playing my guitar and mandolin in coffee shops on Bleecker Street and waiting on people like Janis Joplin and Jimi Hendrix at the Bitter End Cafe." It was an exciting time, but Linda knew that the life of her youth had its limitations and she was ready to get on with her dream of working with animals. She'd try her hardest to get into vet school, but if she didn't get in, she told herself, she was going to Nashville.

After graduating from Brooklyn College, she applied to several schools, but no school would look at a New York resident, or at a woman no less, when New York had its own veterinary college at Cornell. Kansas State University offered her an interview after she took a few prerequisite "aggie courses" there. At the interview she was told, "If we take you then you're going to send a boy to Vietnam by taking his place. Is that fair?" Another interviewer told her that every woman immediately became pregnant upon graduation, essentially wasting the degree. "I envisioned some wind across campus carrying sperm and impregnating all the women," laughs Linda. Her uncle, a KSU veterinarian, kept sending her information on human medical research. For him, vet school for his niece, a girl, wasn't even an option. "The more negativity I got," she continued, "the more I said, 'Look, I'm just going to get in.'"

She applied to Tuskegee thinking that they were going to turn her down because they'd asked for a photo in the admissions packet. Part of her eventual acceptance was based on providing integration for the school, according to Linda, because in order for the university to receive federal funding, they needed to be integrated. Hers was the third class that had white students, and she was the second white woman. Mary Toothman, an equine student, had graduated the year earlier.

She was thrilled to finally get accepted to vet school, but in addition to the overt resentment she experienced from some, she also unwittingly offended others. She'd run into seemingly innocent problems when she used an expression like, "Oh boy," and someone thought she was calling him "boy" derogatorily. The friend who had driven with her to those truck stop lunches, Carolyn Gause Self, now a close confidant, told her, "They're just trying to get you, just trying to scare you. Don't listen to them."

Linda says that Carolyn helped her overcome doubts and challenges. "She was a lot stronger than me," she says. "There was another black classmate who just advised me, 'Ignore them. They're just trying to make you uncomfortable.'" One teacher was blunter and simply told her to keep her mouth shut. "That's become great value advice over the years," she says. "If you keep your mouth shut, they won't know what you are thinking. I'm a little emotional—well, a lot emotional—and I've learned to keep my mouth closed and my emotions in check."

Though she might not have appreciated it at the time, Tuskegee had a history of producing extraordinary leaders. The university's founder, Booker T. Washington, successfully navigated white society, and was the first black man invited to the White House. He was able to straddle black and white societies, and he built an impressive school and that launched other leaders in the black community. His legacy is enormous, reaching well beyond the school's original 1883 charter of the education of "colored" students.

Another distinguishing feature of Tuskegee is that it is built on an ethic of student involvement. The original veterinary buildings were built by the students, brick by brick, according to records. This sense of investment and can-do attitude has permeated the culture and is responsible in part for producing so many leaders over the years, says Linda. Since she graduated, five alumni have gone on to become African American deans of veterinary colleges, a stunning legacy, and many, like Linda, are leaders in organized veterinary medicine as well. "Look at Ted Cohn, of my generation," says Linda about another white student among the first at Tuskegee. "He was just president of the AVMA."

Even if quotas played a role in Tuskegee's decision to accept Linda, the college produced a leader who went on to influence the profession in ways neither Linda nor her alma mater could have anticipated at the time—but first she had the gender obstacle to overcome. Growing up just at the cusp of the women's rights movement made her feel that she was expected give in to the leading man, the way the movie stars of that era like Doris Day did. "It was ingrained in me that the men are the bosses and the leaders, and the women stayed home. My mother had discouraged me from becoming a vet and told me to be a teacher so I could be home during the summers for my future family," she says. Coming of age during the seismic cultural and political shifts of the 1960s, Linda's early attitudes about the role of women shifted radically during this time, too. While she discarded the old mentality during college and vet school, she also learned to keep her new-found voice in check there, a restraint that would serve her later as a leader.

However, on some important issues, her voice was heard loud and clear by faculty, including the professor who had advised her to keep her mouth shut. She thought, for example, that the early administrators directed students away from clinical practice and instead into military, research, the pharmaceutical industry, and meat inspection because they felt that the students couldn't make it as entrepreneurs. Linda spoke up because she believed it shortchanged the black community. "I argued that point to one of the deans and said that the students didn't want to become veterinarians to sit in the laboratory or behind a desk and write grants or serve in the military. But with the difficulty in passing the state boards, they were orienting people away from practice," she says. "Fortunately, that unspoken policy changed."

"Part of that change came from the students speaking out and saying, 'I want to be a practitioner.' I can't say it was the white students more than the black students, but most kids wanted clinical practice," she continues. As the years went by, more students went into practice and also passed the boards. Linda's passion for students' success never dimmed. She later became president of the alumni association, the first woman of any color to hold that position.

When she graduated, she returned to New York to find work. "I managed to dodge the 'impregnating winds' that the Kansas State University admissions committee had warned me about," she says. After leaving one of her first jobs because she didn't agree with the boss, she found herself on the sidewalk holding a box of her belongings. A client approached Linda whose arms were filled and emotions were brimming, asking where she was going. The client desperately wanted Linda to be the doctor to see her cat, pleading with her to continue. She gave the client her number and, launching her home-visit practice right then and there, went to see the cat soon after at its home.

Eventually, she opened an office practice of her own, becoming the first woman to open a vet clinic in Brooklyn. Her parents and aunt supported her in getting started, not just financially, but with the classic Linda Jacobson community spirit. "I remember doing ECG's on the table when we were about the have dinner, and other times hanging the IV from the chandelier. When I had to euthanize a dog, I'd passed my infant daughter to the grieving client to help him through the pain," she says, welling up at the memory. Her parents would offer grieving clients a glass of scotch as well.

As a practice owner, she became successful despite having no family background in business. "I'm a terrible businessperson," she says, and she eventually relied on an office manager. Linda says that her gender has played both a positive and challenging role in her business. "As a woman, I am very compassionate and nurturing, but being a woman has perhaps hurt me also. People would come and find me more caring and nurturing," she says. "But some would come and tell me they could not afford the surgery, and I would tell them to pay me what they could. I would never put an animal to sleep because someone couldn't pay. Some were very appreciative. But the nurturing and compassion helped me as a practitioner as well as building the practice."

As her practice grew, so did her involvement in organized veterinary medicine and her leadership. After a short time being involved in the New York State association, she was assigned a chairmanship and then became a member of the board. Because she was also an association member, she was encouraged by people like Malcolm Kram, mentor to so many including Dr. Lila Miller (below) and Dr. Gail Hansen (described later), pulling her into the PR committee at the state level. She also got involved in the North American Veterinary Community (NAVC) Conference, where she had been nominated to the board and later served as its president. "I think I was the fourth or fifth woman president of NAVC in 2005, but NAVC had its first woman president in 1988," she said, citing its early commitment to women. "Mary Beth Leininger was AVMA president in 1996, and the first woman president of AAHA was after 1988. But NAVC stood apart. They recognized women much earlier."

Linda's warmth and social skills make her an effective committee member, but she might be overly self-effacing when reflecting about her ascension through the officer chairs and then finally president of the New York State association in 2012. "It was almost good for an association to say they had a woman president; it was kind of a novelty," she says, adding that there had been three women presidents before her. One of her triumphs as president of the New York State association "was when I passed the president's gavel to Linda Tintle, the next president, I got a standing ovation from the whole board," she recalls. "They stood up and applauded. Who could ask for more?"

While Linda has taken on leadership roles easily, she always had a little bit of insecurity. Even so, "when my name advanced for a position, I would just say, 'Show me and train me.' I rarely have said 'no' to challenges." However, lately she's beginning to say no for a different reason. Recently, the alternate AVMA House of Delegates representative was resigning and asked Linda to consider running. "I love the AVMA, but I told myself I was too old (not mentally) and that I was getting behind the learning curve on things like social media. Things are moving faster. Now it's someone else's turn," she says. "That was for me a very mature position to take, because I was eminently qualified and people like Ted Cohn are looking for more Tuskegee presence in the profession, so I could have lobbied effectively for myself." Linda practiced leadership generosity in stepping aside and pushing someone else forward. Most trailblazers know their place in history, and Linda knows that she and others in the early years opened up the path for younger women to make it much easier for them. There's no more need for the first woman president of any organization, she says.

As someone who was among the first woman in so many roles, Linda radiates optimism. A true New Yorker, Linda was in Macy's once and saw Mary Beth Leininger, first female president of the AVMA. "I just turned to the saleswoman and said, 'Do you know who this is?'" Linda recalls. She's just as excited about the past as she is about the way the profession is helping to advance women's leadership today.

Looking back, it's easier for Linda to see her own contributions to the profession, but of those years she says, "I never thought of myself as a trail-blazer. All I wanted to do was to become a veterinarian." Thanks to the veterinary college that accepted her when others would not, she followed her dream and opened doors for other women. "That's why Tuskegee has my heart and soul."

Dr. Sylvia Berg Salk

Several decades before Linda Jacobson traveled to Alabama, Sylvia Berg, a bright, young woman from the Catskill region north of New York City, applied to Cornell University in 1941. She was denied. Though women had occasionally been admitted to Cornell in the 1930s, there was heavy bias against them. For one thing, the common assumption was that they would have nothing to offer the agricultural practices that were so strongly rooted in the land-grant mission of the university. Jewish women like Sylvia had an especially difficult time. Sylvia applied the following year, and she was again denied. Frustrated and angry, Sylvia's mother traveled to Cornell and met with the dean. "I know neither the substance nor the tenor of the conversation," Sylvia said years later, "but it must have been interesting because I was admitted the following fall."

Despite being admitted, many faculty and administrators didn't think women should be in veterinary college during the 1940s, and they some-times treated women harshly. Sylvia remembers being assigned an awful, foul-smelling horse carcass to dissect in her first-year anatomy class. "It was poorly embalmed and green with rotten flesh and you couldn't get the stench off your hands or clothes," she recalls. During her clinical year, it was even worse. Male students were assigned a partner to help restrain horses that were being treated after they were castrated, but she was denied assistance and had to control the rope attached to the halter on the head while bending dangerously under the belly to treat the wound. Sylvia never forgot this discriminatory treatment, and it would be sixty years before she returned to Cornell for a class reunion.

She graduated in 1946 and married a classmate, Herman Salk. They moved to Vermont where Sylvia became the state's first female veterinarian. They entered practice with a classmate, Sylvia doing the small animal work while the two men looked after the large animals. After a brief period in which Herman worked in the virology department of Parke Davis Research Laboratory, the Salks moved to a farm in western Pennsylvania where Herman raised laboratory mice for a hundred dollars a month. Sylvia supplemented their income by operating a small animal practice out of their home, using the kitchen table as an operating table.

Those were the days in the early 1950s when Herman's brother, Jonas Salk, was feverishly working at the nearby University of Pittsburgh to develop the eponymous polio vaccine. The children of the two families grew up together and were among the first to be inoculated with the new vaccine.

Eventually, the Salks moved to California where they opened a successful small animal practice. Over the next two decades they became increasingly drawn to humanitarian work, and they began travelling to developing countries where they used their veterinary expertise to help others. They eventually sold their California practice and made their ultimate career move, spending the next several years in Africa and in the Far East. When they finally returned to the United States, they worked with the Navajo and Hopi nations. "We lived under challenging conditions," Sylvia says, "but our work was satisfying. We taught vaccination strategies, production medicine, nutrition, and management. We tried to leave places better than we found them."

In 1990, four and a half decades after graduating with her DVM, Sylvia enrolled in a master's degree program in international public health. As the only veterinarian in the California class, the one with the most international experience, and certainly one of the oldest students, by then in her 60s, she was able to bring a broad perspective to the program, especially in the area of zoonotic diseases. The Salks even developed a scholarship program to support bringing African students to the United States for college education in the health sciences, education, or agriculture. Dozens of students benefited from the program, including a young Masai woman who became the first woman from her tribe to pursue an advanced degree.

The challenges for contemporary women, while tempered by modern attitudes, opportunities, and laws, are still formidable, but it's easy to forget what it was like only two or three generations ago when very few women were even allowed access to veterinary medicine. Thanks to trailblazers like Sylvia, whose persistence and success paid off despite tough odds, women today are standing on their shoulders and reaping the benefit of opportunities they helped create.

Dr. Rachel Cezar

An impressive early career veterinarian, Dr. Rachel Cezar's path to veterinary medicine has many parallels to the experiences of nonminority women who entered the profession fifty years ago. Rachel grew up in a small rural Michigan town with parents who expected her to graduate from high school, get a good job, and then get married and have children. They didn't understand her dream of becoming a veterinarian, and they discouraged her when they learned that it would be an eight-year process. While challenging at the time, she says that the bumpy path ultimately prepared her for the greater challenges ahead. As a petite woman of color and a first-generation college student whose goal it was to work with large animals, Rachel's trajectory wasn't easy.

"I started very early in this sector of veterinary medicine and was told over and over again that I needed to be more clinically seasoned to be in certain positions," says Rachel. "However, I was able to prove them wrong and continue my career path forward." She learned to draw on the determination she honed in the face of her parents' initial lack of support and developed a personal motto. "Against all odds" plays in her head as a reminder of the times when "even your family doesn't believe in your dreams." When Rachel uses her characteristic inspirational statements, they never sound trite. "You need to continue to push through those hardships," she says. "You need to take the hardships as lessons learned so you can keep thriving in the beloved career and path you have chosen."

Perseverance often comes at a cost, especially for those who feel they are representing their gender, class, or race, and who are acutely aware of being a "first"—the first in their family to go to college, the first woman of color in the position, and so forth. Being a leader of the National Horse Protection Program was stressful as well as rewarding. Rachel found that working in animal welfare was very high-profile, and working in government demanded constant explanations to Congress. It was a level of limelight and pressure that she wasn't used to, and it took its toll physically. After two years in the post she was diagnosed with a debilitating disease. It was a wake-up call. After learning to take care of herself emotionally and physically, she got well. "Fortunately," she says, "I was able to continue moving the program forward and decrease the abuse of these horses as well as keep my sanity by not sweating the small or big things anymore."

Giving has been one way for Rachel to bring greater balance to her life. She volunteers at her alma mater, Michigan State University, in their summer program for college students. The MSU College of Veterinary Medicine Vetward Bound program targets first-generation college students who are interested in veterinary medicine and who are educationally, economically, and/or culturally disadvantaged. She tells students that financing an education is possible, demonstrating that she's a living example of that. She helps students understand that there are opportunities outside working in a clinic that can support their financial goals, and that they have a nice lifestyle while working in the profession.

She, like others, believe that the veterinary profession could improve economically if the profession better reflected American society. "The inclusion of more people of color broadens the profession to represent our society, and that will potentially increase access to health care for pets by clients who will feel more comfortable looking for specific kinds of providers from their own background," she says. "Having more diversity potentially can also increase access to animal health in various parts of the world, especially the developing world."

Rachel's definition of diversity in veterinary medicine is broad, including the diversity of fields that are available to aspiring veterinarians, including military, government, research, academia, and even Congress. Having engaged with the Animal Welfare Committee of the AVMA and the American Association of Equine Practitioners (AAEP), and more recently as president-elect of the Women's Veterinary Leadership Development Initiative, she's able to pursue her passion for diversity in a wider sense.

"I believe this is the beginning pathway for our veterinary leadership to begin embracing diversity as a whole," she says, "and I look forward to the future and supporting the venues to enhance diversity in our profession."

Now that Rachel has greater balance in her life personally and has become a new mother, it might be time for a new motto. "Against all odds" tells her story up to this point. It will be up to her to imagine the rest of her life and the impact she'll have on others.

Dr. Ruby Perry

As a young girl, Dr. Ruby Perry witnessed her mother's passion and her unrelenting commitment to the civil rights movement. By her words and actions, Ruby's mother indirectly "charted [her] life" by pushing her to take a leap of faith to make a difference toward the common good. Her mother always said it was her responsibility to use the gifts she had been given for civil rights. Ruby's mother comes through her, with a direct gaze and sentences that bridge inspiration and common sense.

As the middle child of five, Ruby felt "boxed-in," and that pushed her toward developing a spirit of independence. Though her siblings received the same opportunities for an education, Ruby's mother perceived that she was different. She was highly inquisitive by nature, and she had a desire to explore the world and its opportunities. Ruby's mother encouraged her, putting her in a typing class that eventually helped her through college. Though she would have preferred playing basketball like other children, she says, "I got cut in the first round anyway, so my mother's decision turned out to be a fortuitous one."

"I grew up in the Deep South in the small Mississippi town called Tougaloo, right across the street from a historically black college by the same name," she says. "The college served as the base for gatherings and meetings of civil rights leaders visiting my area. The local community, of which my mother was a prominent member, provided refuge and food for the leaders, and supported their plans and their strategies to advance desegregation."

The defining event in Ruby's teenage life was becoming one of the students chosen by her mother and other community leaders, in collaboration with local civil rights leaders, to officially desegregate the high school adjacent to the neighborhood where she lived. "I was pulled from my segregated high school in Jackson, Mississippi, to be one of five African American students to enter the tenth grade in an all-white high school," she says. The five students were unwelcome both subtly and directly, and had no social interaction with their white classmates, yet they all survived to graduation. They maintained no association with the school whatsoever until 2009 when they were unexpectedly invited to their fortieth class reunion. Two of the five had died and a third couldn't be located. Only Ruby and one other former student attended what turned out to be an emotional conclusion to an untenable forty-year estrangement.

"Many of my classmates remembered what we had endured and came up to us and apologized," she remembers. "The former school principal was even there, and he made a special effort to meet with us to talk about those three years at his high school during the height of the civil rights movement. He also expressed remorse for how we had been treated by him and by others on his watch. The choir director, who had refused to allow us to join the school choir when we were in high school, invited us to sing in the class reunion choir. It was an extraordinary event," she says, emotions choking her usually clear voice.

"My journey involved risks," she says, recalling her mother's admonition to seize the moment whenever it presented itself. "Because you are black," her mother told her, "and because you are growing up in rural Mississippi in this civil rights era, you will only get an opportunity once. Don't let it pass you by." Her mother used her own gifts in the cause, and Ruby would use her gifts in veterinary medicine.

Her trajectory started with her mother's words. She finished high school during those turbulent years, and then she went on to Tuskegee University and graduated from the veterinary college in 1977. She received a master of science degree from Michigan State University in 1991 and became a board-certified radiologist and member of the American College of Veterinary Radiology. Finally, Ruby returned to Tuskegee University in 2015 to become the first female dean of the College of Veterinary Medicine, Nursing and Allied Health.

Along the way, taking risks and seizing opportunities, relying on mentors and friends to give honest feedback, Ruby carries on her mother's legacy. She asks, admonishes, and inspires those around her to take risks and work hard for the cause. Her cause, not just her career, is veterinary medicine, and her students are the people who will lead it.

Dr. Lila Miller

Growing up in Harlem in the 1950s and 1960s, Dr. Lila Miller knew at an early age that she was special. Teachers and adults kept telling her that she was smart, that she was headed for something exceptional. An aunt told her mother that she'd better get a job because "this one's going to college and you're going to need money to send her there." With a five-year-old's dream of wanting to be a vet despite never having seen one, she showed promise and was placed in an elementary school program run by City College, receiving a public school education with the quality of private school.

At Hunter College High School for the intellectually gifted in Manhattan, she was the only African American student in her class. Because she had to prove everyone right, that she was special and smart, all she did was study. She felt burdened by their expectations. "I was bright and blessed as a child, but that also put a certain pressure on me because people said, 'Ok, you're really smart, show us what you can do.' I never got that pressure from my parents," she says. She says that as a kid she was the nerd and didn't have many friends.

"My best friend was my dog," she says. Her parents had gotten the animal at the ASPCA. One day she returned home from school to awful news. Her parents had taken her dog back to the ASPCA because he had been sick. Later, her mother told her that someone at the organization had called and said that the dog had died and that the family needed to come pay the bill and collect his body. Lila became hysterical and distraught, a completely unfamiliar girl to her parents. Her father promised they'd get another dog, but her mother said something different.

"No. You're not getting another dog," she said. "You need human friends. You have no people skills; go down to the YWCA and make some friends!" That advice turned out to hold more wisdom than her mother could have imagined. Lila became involved in the organization, and at a time when the national board was looking for input from teenagers, she traveled to Texas with a special group. She helped form a national teen organization and became its first cochairperson. The YWCA changed their bylaws, she says, so she could be a voting member on their national board because she was too young. The organization was a leader in addressing racism, and she traveled and volunteered with them extensively. That organization became Lila's first mentor besides her mother.

"I don't think I could've gotten through Cornell without their support," she says. She'd needed large animal experience as an admission requirement, but a prospective student from Harlem couldn't find that. The ladies at the YWCA told her that they knew someone who ran a summer camp in Beacon, New York, and that working on the farm there would qualify for the large animal experience. "They held my hand," she says. They would also help her through some of her darkest times once at Cornell.

As an undergraduate, she experienced more internal pressure than she'd experienced in high school. She felt that she needed to be the very best so that the college wouldn't have any excuse to turn her away. "Everything I did at Cornell had that pressure. I can't be mediocre, I can't be acceptable, I've got to be better," she says. And she challenged bias. When put in a remedial math and science program simply because she was African American, she said, "I took advanced placement biology at Hunter College and you're putting me in beginner's biology? Have you seen my [New York State Board of] Regents' exam scores or high school transcript?"

The 1970s were a different era for women and certainly for African Americans in veterinary colleges. In 1973, Lila and Rochelle Woods were the first African American women to be admitted to Cornell's veterinary college. Academically, Lila proved herself, but the challenges of overcoming biases and prejudice were enormous, and she developed an allergy to horses so severe that after an almost near fatal asthma attack, she had to constantly take medications because classes were held in the barn. The pressure and the side effects from medications were exhausting.

At one point, she considered leaving the college, quitting, but Dean Ed Melby said they would not let any more African American students in the veterinary college if she ended up quitting. She and Rochelle were an "experiment," he said. "If you drop out," Lila remembers him saying, "you'll be a statistic. They won't know or care why you left, so how can you expect other blacks to be admitted?"

The YWCA women mentored her along the way, framing her experiences as institutional racism rather than bias targeted at her as an individual, and they helped her choose her battles. "These YW people were white and helped me keep my eyes on the prize," Lila says. "I had personal relationships with these women, including a lobbyist who was talking about global, data-driven issues on racism. They helped me understand what I was experiencing in a larger context." She found support on campus as well. Dan Tapper, professor of physiology and well-known for his empathy for social issues like racism and sexism, was sympathetic and offered support to Lila and Rochelle.

She graduated from the veterinary college in 1977, truly at the end of her resolve. "I thought, I don't care anymore; I've proved my point, there's nothing more that I need to do," she recalls. She was angry and bitter, and her whole life's dream was hanging in the balance. She did pass the New York State Board, "wearing an army gas mask because they gave the exam in the barn." She was tired. "When I graduated, I was done," she continues. "I didn't understand why the profession fought me when I just wanted to go back to Harlem and help poor people take care of their pets." She entertained becoming a travel agent or working for the YWCA instead of treating animals.

A remarkable man reeled her back to her childhood dream of being a veterinarian. Dr. Joseph Lloyd Tait, a University of Pennsylvania graduate from Jamaica, was practicing in Harlem. She had met him during her college years. Back then, she had never stepped into a veterinarian's office and had never even met a vet. "I'd been trying to get small animal experience, calling every vet in the phone book and going down the alphabet," says Lila. "I was discouraged because I was already down to the T's without any luck. I got him on the phone and asked if I could come over and he said he didn't have any work."

Hearing her voice on the phone, he asked if she was a sister (African American). Lila said yes, and he said to come on over right away, she remembers. "I didn't even know if he was black. If I had realized there were black veterinarians in Harlem, I would've started there," she laughs. At the time, Dr. Tait said that he didn't have any work for Lila, but he arranged for her to work at the practice of a good friend of his, Harold Zweighaft. She worked for a couple of summers there, dividing divided her time between Drs. Tait and Zweighaft, and met "another very nice vet, Dr. Malcom Kram."

Lila says that that Dr. Tait didn't understand her bitterness because they'd embraced him as a student at the University of Pennsylvania. As a black man from the West Indies whose experiences of racism were radically different than hers, he became the mentor who told her to get over her bitterness. "Pick and choose your battles, cover your back," he said repeatedly. "Life is not fair, Lila, grow up. There's nothing in the contract that says things have to be fair." She had hoped that Cornell was an isolated experience and that all she had to do was get back to Harlem for circumstances to improve. Dr. Tait told her this wasn't the reality.

He also exposed her to the underserved animals in shelters, those that didn't get attention in vet school, the animals that would shape her career and distinguish her as a leader. Dr. Tait was an advisor to ASPCA, and she used to go with him to visit the shelters. "The shelters were awful," she says. "I thought, 'I don't want anything to do with this.'" But Dr. Tait said that the animals needed Lila, and he needed her, and he was persistent.

She worked in the ASPCA shelters for five years. They were using the decompression chamber for euthanasia when she got there, but they soon switched over to euthanasia by IV injection. She was instrumental in training others in this and other procedures, realizing that other shelter veterinarians and staff could help each other and share information. She saw the need to write an internal operations manual to help other vets at their locations. The ASPCA gave her a two-week sabbatical for the project. "I was writing it for myself and immediate staff," she says, "but the ASPCA incorporated it into their overall operations manual." The manual would be the beginning of a greater project.

After five years of shelter work and euthanizing, she was ready for something else. Dr. Tait had been trying to get her to take over his practice, but she didn't want what she described as the headaches that she'd seen him deal with. The ASPCA was planning to open a clinic in Brooklyn, and he wanted her to run it.

"I thought no," she remembers. "I can't do it because I haven't had clinical experience and it's been five years since vet school." The practice was in east New York, Brooklyn, one of the worst areas in the city with the highest murder rates. Dr. Tait proved persuasive and supportive once again, but he drove a hard bargain. He said he'd support her but that she had to make it work as a business because the ASPCA would shut it down if it didn't at least break even. Lila ran the clinic for fifteen years, from 1982–1997.

Dr. Tait also helped her expand beyond shelter medicine, exposing her to the State Board, one of the most powerful influences in veterinary medicine in New York that deals with licensing, complaints, and malpractice charges. "One reason I didn't want to get involved in organized vet med because it was all white men, but Dr. Tait said that they needed smart people, women, and people of color. I also didn't want to join the board because some of those meetings were back at Cornell," says Lila.

"The board mellowed me out a little," she recalls. "The power was all with white men, but they didn't all fit my stereotype of what I thought they'd be. I liked working with Ellsworth Thorndyke and Lew Watson— that made me less bitter." What she really wanted to do was to get rid of the New York State Board exam. She felt that there was a serious bias problem because it was a face-to-face practical exam administered by private practitioners with strong personal prejudices. She cast the deciding vote on abolishing the exam. "We thought the Regents were going to get rid of it anyway," she says, "but I got a call saying you have to come to this meeting to break the impending tie vote." She eventually became chair of the board.

"I even got a plaque saying that I had reviewed more disciplinary cases than anyone in the history of the board. I wanted to dispel the attitude I felt people still held that black folks are lazy, so I always wanted to review all cases promptly and well," she recalls.

After fifteen years, the Brooklyn ASPCA clinic closed in 1997. It was a crossroads for Lila. What other career option did she have? The science advisor at the ASPCA, Dr. Stephen Zawistowski, said there were no veterinarians to answer medical questions from the public and he needed someone to fill that role. She took the job because he thought she could do it. The first thing he asked her to do was to organize a "dangerous dog conference," and later introduced her to Dr. Jan Scarlett, who encouraged her to teach a course on shelter medicine at Cornell. He said they could combine Scarlett's teaching skills with her own knowledge of shelter medicine. Lila said that she didn't want anything to do with teaching at Cornell, but Dr. Tait's voice came back to her, saying, "Let it go. Get over it."

Lila and Dr. Scarlett became close colleagues. It was Dr. Scarlett who nominated Lila for the Cornell Salmon Award for Distinguished Alumni Service, which she received in 2014. The first residency program in shelter medicine started at the University of California, Davis. Kate Hurley at Davis called Lila to tap her expertise, and with the Cornell course and now the residency program, the field was gaining legitimacy. Shelter medicine was approved as a board specialty in 2014.

"I never set out to make a career in shelter medicine; I never imagined this direction," Lila says, shaking her head. She has coedited the first two texts on shelter medicine, *Shelter Medicine for Veterinarians and Staff* and *Infectious Disease Management in Animal Shelters,* and she still teaches at Cornell, the alma mater that she almost quit, and at the University of Pennsylvania, the alma mater of Dr. Tait, who drew her back to the profession that she has unquestionably influenced.

Takeaway Tips

- If you're in a position to admit, hire, or advance others, take a risk. Take a chance on people who might not have the complete package of skills up front. By allowing people to enter from different routes and by focusing on core qualities instead of just essential skills, you could end up nurturing a future leader who will not only build personal success, but will improve veterinary medicine as a whole. It's not an act of charity to encourage diversity, but an act of change.

- Strong, outspoken women are used to pushback and critique of their directness. Don't change your qualities, but know when it's strategic and wise to monitor your outspokenness in order to get things done. Like Dr. Linda Jacobson, learn to listen in the situations when it will be more efficacious for advancing your goals.

- When you're the first in your family or the first of your group to achieve access and success, the pressures are enormous, as they were for Drs. Rachel Cezar and Lila Miller. Seek friends and mentors to help you find balance, manage stress, and stay healthy. Being a trailblazer helps those behind you, but don't let forging new terrain damage yourself in the process.

- Like Dr. Ruby Perry's mother admonished her, you will only get an opportunity once. Don't let it pass you by.

- Know when it's time to push someone else forward. Like Dr. Linda Jacobson, who decided to say no to people who encouraged her to run for another AVMA position, practice leadership generosity and pass an opportunity onto someone else.

Notes

1.   Marianne Schnall, "An Interview with Maya Angelou," *Psychology Today*, February 17, 2009, https://www.psychologytoday.com/blog/the-guest-room/200902/interview-maya-angelou.

2.   Association of American Veterinary Medical Colleges, "Recruitment," http://www.aavmc.org/Programs-and-Initiatives/Recruitment.aspx.

4

Career Changers and the Several Year Switch

Most girls who grow up dreaming of becoming a veterinarian start out imagining a future of mending dogs, cats, and horses. They picture themselves making tough diagnoses and offering life-saving treatments while grateful owners become loyal clientele. Valerie Ragan achieved that dream, thriving happily in a small animal clinic for five years. But after a routine of working in the same small animal practice, at the same building, and performing routine cat spays, she realized that life in practice was starting to become all too familiar. She was bored. Raised overseas, she craved something more out but didn't know what the something was. It's hard to imagine Valerie bored. She crackles with enthusiasm and describes things in the big picture, moving her arms in wide circles, smiling just as wide, and making you feel like you were about to have the same brilliant idea.

One night during clinic duties, she was waiting for an emergency case to arrive. A dog had been hit by a car and the owners were bringing it in after hours. It was late, she felt dull, and to stay awake before the patient arrived, she began flipping through a pamphlet. She saw pictures of veterinarians working outdoors, something she had been longing for. She saw pictures of veterinarians on airplanes, something she dreamed of. There were pictures of veterinarians in foreign countries working side by side with different kinds of people, something missing from her life after growing up abroad. She saw all this in a government pamphlet that happened to be left in a pile.

Veterinarians sing the praises of their flexible profession, celebrating the array of opportunities in this wide field. Mixed animal practice is satisfying, and so is a career in public health. How about government service? Do you love research? Teaching? Industry? All of the above? For the veterinarian who thrives on change, this career seems made for her.

Fortunately, veterinarians have the advantage of working in a profession that offers a vast landscape of career options. The versatility of a DVM, like a passport, allows veterinarians to explore new options across the globe, and to lead in them. The American Association of Veterinary Medical Colleges and virtually all veterinary colleges exalt the myriad directions open to students. The AVMA, acknowledging that almost 28 percent of veterinarians in clinical practice eventually consider transitioning to a nonclinical career, offers programming to help clinicians shift to research or researchers shift to industry.[1] It wasn't always this way in veterinary medicine or other occupations.

Switching careers might be common now,[2] but not that long ago workers in all professions stayed with one career, even one job, for most of their working life. The social contract rewarded employee loyalty with stability, 401Ks, and gold watches after fifty years of service, and the culture valued people who stayed in a single position while judging sternly those who flitted from one job to another.

Today a mishmash of generations, genders, races, and backgrounds crowd the workplace, as do colliding values and assumptions.[3] Now, changing careers is accepted and even encouraged across generations. Articles abound with success stories of people in their second and third acts: a forty-something woman who left a successful CEO position to become a psychotherapist; a fifty-five-year-old woman who started medical school. Celebrating change as part of a long and vibrant life, professional coaches, books, and even the Stanford Distinguished Careers Institute[4] are part of the growing economy around these career changers. No longer the company man or woman because the companies of the past don't keep employees for their entire lives anymore, older workers are adapting the mobility mentality of their younger cohorts and reinventing themselves.[5]

Staying in one place works well for some personalities and generations, but moving every few years is actually advised by some experts. Vivian Giang says in a *Fast Company* article, "You should plan on switching careers every three years for the rest of your life,"[6] and insists that job hoppers learn fast, make good impressions, and improve the bottom line quickly. Patti McCord, former chief talent officer for Netflix and career consultant, told Giang that people build skills faster when changing companies because they're more practiced at the learning curve.

Giang also interviewed Penelope Trunk, author of *Brazen Careerist: The New Rules for Success*, who says that people used to think that the longer you kept an employee, the more worth they developed for the boss, because you train them, they get used to their job, and then they do it. "But, in fact," she says, "an employee who stays on the job and isn't learning at a really high rate is not as engaged, so they're not doing as good work. So it turns out, the employee who stays longest, you get the least work out of, and the employees that job hunt are the most receptive of becoming extremely useful, very fast."[7]

Trunk believes that the learning curve "pretty much flattens after three years." While there are few exceptions to jobs people should stay in for longer, such as academia, most people should leave if they want to stay engaged, she says.

This isn't to say that professionals who stay in the same position or with the same organizations aren't less energized or are less effective leaders than career changers. The fortunate people who discovered what they wanted to do early on and stuck with it are simply a different breed of leader than the career-changing leaders. Veterinarians seeking the several year switch stay engaged by moving around. "It was good for me, and I believe it's also good for the profession," says Ralph Richardson, reflecting on his seven-year pattern of changing positions. He made this point toward the end of his long career while delivering the Recognition Lecture at the 2016 AAVMC Annual Meeting.

Career change, while stimulating for people who crave it and good for the profession in general, can present challenges to employers who haven't adapted for it in their business plans. This is especially true for small practice owners, as well as for their clients who expect to see the same veterinarian they've come to trust. These are major challenges for the veterinary profession, and one that industry professionals are trying to address in order to keep veterinary practices vibrant.[8]

Low threshold for routine[9] and high desire for challenge is part of the make up of veterinarians on the move, as is confidence and an appetite for risk-taking. Watch children on a playground and it's easy to tell who embodies the risk-taking phenotype, but harder to spot are *future* adults who will cultivate this quality through practice and intention. Whether innate or learned, these qualities seem to be strong indicators of career changers.

The three women's stories in this chapter illustrate their commonalities in government service and epidemiology, yet despite being risk-takers all, their life paths reveal choices as unique as they are. One launched a career as an international expert in brucellosis; one became a commander in federal disaster preparedness; and one became a state epidemiologist. Each has sought opportunities and seized those that seemed to have dropped out of the sky.

Dr. Valerie Ragan

If Valerie hadn't been trying to stay awake in the clinic that night while waiting for the injured dog (who recovered just fine), she probably wouldn't have read the pamphlet about the United States Department of Agriculture (USDA) careers. All she'd known about government veterinarians up until then was that that they worked in meat inspection.

Valerie had never had problem with risk-taking; she just did it in her own style—prepare, take a risk, jump in. She prepared for the switch to the USDA work by polishing up her cow skills, rereading large animal texts from veterinary school, and hanging out at the sale barns. She told herself that if she got the job, she'd give it at least one year. She got the job.

"Anyone can learn the technical stuff, but it's the people skills that make candidates truly invaluable," she says. It's easy to imagine her saying this to the students she counsels today, and because of her genuine concern for them, it's easy to imagine them listening. Valerie radiates warmth, and she articulates her ideas in full paragraphs, like someone who is comfortable with her own intelligence and assumes that of others. She exhibits no pretense at all and listens carefully before offering her opinion.

Growing up, Valerie moved with her family in the US Foreign Service to different countries, and the skills she learned then helped her navigate—and eventually lead—in an array of very different veterinary posts. She works around the world with farmers, ministers of agriculture, deans, and students, giving presentations to hundreds in auditoriums or teaching a rural veterinarian outdoors how to educate ranchers about brucellosis. Her success comes in part from her philosophy that while rank and role are fluid, a person's character is not. "I was raised overseas most of my life," she says, "and my parents drove home to us that you treat everyone with respect regardless of their job or the status that they were born into, whether president or gardener. The reality is that a person that you hire could be your boss someday, especially if you've developed them properly. Today they may be dean or prime minister and tomorrow they may not. You respect the role, but more importantly you respect the person."

The one-year commitment she'd given herself at the USDA turned out to be a seventeen-year career. The original pamphlet she'd flipped through promised opportunities to grow, meet new people, travel, and work outside, and Valerie took full advantage of all that. During those years she moved into different roles, as epidemiology officer and up the administrative chain, learning and growing. Eventually, though, she missed the hands-on work with ranchers and the fieldwork when she trained veterinarians on brucellosis prevention and treatment.

After seventeen years, she decided that she could make a go of a consulting company doing the outdoor work with international ranchers, so she launched AgWorks Solutions. Again, this was done in Valerie style: prepare, take a risk, jump in. She spent six months developing a business plan, reading business books, interviewing other veterinarians turned business consultants, and she learned everything from assessing her competition to building clients to setting income goals. Her USDA friends asked how she could leave a good government organization and be brave enough to go out on her own. She insists that she felt totally prepared by the time she made the jump. "I'm not going to jump ship and tread water until I figure it out," she says. "I take risks, but very calculated risks. Part of my comfort is to stretch, but stretch safely. Maybe I over prepare, but that's what builds confidence for me."

She switched careers again in 2009, and today Valerie serves as director of the Center for Public and Corporate Veterinary Medicine (CPCVM) at Virginia-Maryland College of Veterinary Medicine, where she makes sure that students have a much greater knowledge of career options than she'd had as a student. For someone who has taken risks and who has explored the globe, Valerie could have written the motto at CPCVM: "The world is our clinic."

Dr. Heather Case

Dr. Heather Case is an energetic woman, the kind of a person you'd meet in a café and within a minute feel like you are friends. Blond, blue-eyed, and wholesome-looking, she could be the poster girl for Minnesota Nice—the famed quality that offers not just directions to a traveler, but a ride and a follow-up call to make sure the person had a good time.

A 1998 graduate of the University of Minnesota, Heather, just like Valerie Ragan, had thought that government veterinarians only did meat inspection. She learned of the true opportunities not through a pamphlet left on a desk, but through a manner that was almost as serendipitous. She had worked for six years as a mixed animal practitioner, and she was developing an itch for a change when she saw an ad from the Minnesota Veterinary Medical Association (VMA) calling for early practitioners to attend the AVMA Veterinary Leadership Conference. Heather learned that the Minnesota VMA had already selected their recent graduate for the conference, but she decided to call anyway. The staffer on the other end of the phone said they would make an extra space for her, all expenses paid. That's when her world changed.

After being out of the networking loop for six years, she went to the conference and met people who introduced her to leaders who in turn kept introducing her to others. Her idea of what public health was expanded with each introduction. "I met a woman veterinarian who was the food safety officer for Coca Cola. Wow, that's not the kind of public health I knew about," she remembers. At the conference she learned about a residency program in public health at the University of Minnesota. It was fifty miles away from where she lived, she had a steady job in a practice, and she owned the horse farm she'd always dreamed of, but by September of that year she started her residency in preventive medicine and began working on her master's degree in public health.

An opportunist in the very best sense of the word, the veterinary career changer actually considers prospects that just happen to come along, even if they're crazy and not at all part of her grand plan. While she doesn't look for constant change, she likes taking risks—they make her feel invigorated and remind her that she's growing. Heather was definitely growing. Part of that growth meant learning that she could stretch for positions and opportunities that seemed out of bounds, beyond what she *should* reach for if she played it safe.

When the Minnesota VMA called Heather during her residency and asked her to run for a contested seat on their board, she agreed, despite being a busy resident in public health with a daily commute of a hundred miles. Learning to be comfortable being uncomfortable provided quick payback. She was elected to the VMA post and right away began making an impact.

"I had been an equine vet doing dentistry and all of the sudden a bill to the state legislature comes up on equine dentistry," she says. "We're at the Hill at the state legislature talking to lawmakers, and it really circled back to my interest in talking to clients about heartworm disease and other public health issues. Now I was translating that to someone who is making a law that impacts my profession, and that really energized me." That seed in public policy would begin to sprout soon.

Inside her Minnesota Nice, Heather was growing into someone who considered all opportunities seriously. Her résumé, like all who have career restlessness, started to look like a patchwork of fascinating experiences stitched together by her drive to learn and, quite often, to influence. In addition to her full-time residency while serving as representative of the VMA, she pursued a new opportunity with the AVMA's Veterinary Medical Assistance Team (VMAT) program. She also applied to the AVMA's Governmental Relations Division as part of her master's degree field experience that focused on leadership and public policy. Now she was an equine vet pursuing a master's in public health, on her way to board certification in preventive medicine, about to go to the nation's capital to learn about governmental relations, while signing up to be on a disaster relief team with VMAT. It was a lot, but doing a lot was her new normal, and all was falling into place. Then, Hurricane Katrina hit.

Things move quickly in disaster relief, and Heather was rapidly appointed as the shelter medicine commander of Katrina, stunning herself. She hadn't thought of herself as a commander, but once someone showed that kind of faith in her she had to believe it herself; however, there wasn't a lot of time to reflect on her new position. She shipped out to Louisiana and began rescue and treatment of animals, managing the medical staff and making sure all animals received proper care.

On one of the hottest days about three weeks into the mission, a dog presented in terrible shape with a fever of 109°. As she moved toward the dog, Heather realized that a National Geographic Society film crew was approaching and had been following the dog's case from its initial rescue. Her team immediately went to work saving this dog. Nearly lost in the shuffle of all the excitement, she noticed a couple off to the side. They'd had four dogs before the disaster and had only found three of the four. As her team worked on the critical dog, Heather walked over to talk with the couple. They described their dog and she immediately wondered if she could possibly be another dog that they'd held in an observation cage.

"This dog had arrived for an examination and while she was in pretty good shape physically, we could tell she was older and wanted to monitor her for a while," Heather remembers. "As I walked the couple over to the cage, they burst into relieved tears. The dog we were carefully watching was in fact their beloved pet, Lilly, and she turned out to be fifteen years old. Those were the kinds of cases that kept us going during some really tough times."

There's no single path to leadership. Everyone charts their courses with planned choices, unplanned opportunities, and a little luck. Heather had delayed applying for an externship at the AVMA to be part of Katrina, and afterward she returned to Minnesota after her residency.

It would have been natural for Heather to stay in her home state. She had left a practice and owned a ten-acre horse farm with a stallion and mares. She even had a job offer in public health. "I had it all set and things were neat and tidy," says Heather, but she thought a lot about an AVMA

Congressional Fellowship she had left during Katrina and remembered the public policy seed that she'd tucked away earlier. She thought, "It's now or never. I'm going to take the dice and roll it." She applied for and got the fellowship.

Heather loved Washington, DC, and thought she'd stay after the fellowship, but she kept hearing about a job—a perfect fit, everyone said—in Illinois, at the AVMA. "Finally you hear it enough times and you think, ok, what *is* this?" she says. She applied for the AVMA post as the National Coordinator of Emergency Preparedness and Response, interviewing not because she thought she'd get the job, but because she thought it would be a good learning experience simply to interview. Plus, she was passionate about this work, having lived through Katrina. "I knew that was a calling," she says, "that I was supposed to be working in this, and to have a job in disaster preparedness just seemed ideal."

Career changers, like entrepreneurs, seem infused with self-assuredness. Heather's parents had a lot to do with her confidence. Both were raised on dairy farms in rural Minnesota, working hard and paying their way through college. Her mother had an illness during much of Heather's youth, and it profoundly shaped her confidence and determination to take on new opportunities because she realized early that life is not infinite. "My mother couldn't pursue all of her dreams, so I decided I'm going to go for it," says Heather.

On her most recent decision to leave the AVMA and go to the National Board of Veterinary Medical Examiners as its executive director, she says she did a lot of soul-searching and played out different scenarios. "I loved the AVMA job. It was fabulous, it was safe, I knew what I was doing, and I was making an impact, but I knew I wasn't growing and stretching, so as much as it would've been comfortable to stay at AVMA, I knew I couldn't," she says.

Even now that she's an executive director, Heather still looks for ways to grow. Taking advantage of the associations of executives and CEOs, she goes to meetings to make connections and learn. She also is the one teaching the younger veterinarians about Minnesota Nice, taking them around and making introductions, telling them that they'd be great for this fellowship or that job, sharing her belief in them, and above all else, telling them that change is good.

Dr. Gail Hansen

Sitting at a glass table within the glass offices of the Pew Charitable Trusts in Washington, DC, Dr. Gail Hansen maintains calm confidence, never seeming distracted by the well-dressed men and women who hustle past the fishbowl meeting space. Designed to project transparency, the glass office leaves a visitor feeling like a mouse on a prairie, but not for Gail. As a woman whose grandmother grew up on a farm and didn't have the opportunity for a high school education or travel, Gail is the midwestern girl who went east, then west, then east again.

After graduating from the University of Minnesota, Gail headed east without a flicker of hesitation and joined a small animal practice in Manhattan. The practice owner, Dr. Malcolm Kram, was taking a year to pursue the AVMA Congressional Fellowship, leaving Gail to run the busy practice. It was late 1980s, the height of the AIDS crisis, and Dr. Kram had many gay clients.

A Manhattan man owned a very old poodle that was declining, and Gail, never one to shy from the truth, told him that it was time to put the dog down. She recommended that he not be present for the euthaniz-ing, but the owner insisted, saying that he had been there when the dog was born and he would be there when she had to leave this world. "It was emotional for him and he was crying," Gail says, "so I gave him a Kleenex and a hug." He said that she was the first person to touch him since his lover died of AIDS. His next comment—"My physician won't touch me without gloves"—was a watershed moment and pointed her in the direction of something she'd always considered: public health.

A lot of people in that era had misconceptions about animals and humans with AIDS, and thought that the animals would bring an early death because of zoonotic diseases. Gail knew that there were many unknowns about AIDS and animals, and she thought that someone should be working on the issue and finding out more. That person could be her. Back when Gail was a veterinary student, Dr. Shirley Johnston, who would later become the first female dean at the University of Minnesota, had counseled her to work in practice for a few years before going into public health. Twelve years had passed since graduation, and Gail knew she was ready to make that switch.

As with Drs. Ragan and Case, chance also played a part in her new direction. She and her husband were headed to Malaysia for his work, and they needed to move to the state of Washington to get their affairs in order. There were bureaucratic delays, so while waiting in Seattle for the move, she applied to the School of Public Health at the University of Washington. The Malaysia trip didn't materialize, she got in to school, and she joined only one other veterinarian in the program. After her research in HIV in the Seattle area population, she became an epidemiologist who oversaw interviews at needle exchange sites, prisons, and methadone clinics. Gail loved the work but couldn't shake the idea of who she had been: a veterinarian from the Midwest first and then the East Coast.

"I thought, what do I know about drug users and injectors? I'm a middle-aged white lady," she said. Her misconceptions fell away and her views expanded about intravenous drug users. She learned who they were as people and listened to their stories while tracking their patterns as an epidemiologist.

At the Seattle Department of Public Health, the woman who hired Gail out of graduate school was a veterinarian, PhD, and epidemiologist named Noreen Harris. "She was a brilliant woman," says Gail. There were already four other veterinarians with public health degrees working in the city's public health department, an unusual number, but Dr. Harris didn't care about perceptions as long as she had a strong team. Six months after Gail started, Dr. Harris was killed in a car crash on her way home. Everyone was devastated. Gail's graduate advisor and mentor, Russ Alexander, supported the team. "Even though she had been PhD epidemiologist and the rest of us were master's epis," says Gail, "we had Russ to help us through." He became her lifelong mentor.

After three years, Gail was ready for a change. She was happy and had been working occasional weekends in animal clinics to keep her hands in the field, but she missed veterinary medicine. Seeing that Kansas was looking for a state veterinarian, she decided to interview there. Russ nudged her to fly. "Selfishly I want to keep you here, but the best thing for you is to go off and do something else," she recalls him saying. She applied because of his advice not to get pigeonholed as the HIV epidemiologist.

She and her family moved to Kansas in 1996, and she became the senior epidemiologist and public health veterinarian with the Kansas Department of Health and Environment. "I also was the liaison with Department of Agriculture in Kansas and USDA, the animal health department, wildlife, and parks—wherever there was any kind of animal thing, I was the focal point," she says. The job provided the new learning opportunities she'd sought, and when the state epidemiologist left, she was appointed to the top position. Soon she was able to practice mentoring generosity that had been modeled by Russ. The Centers for Disease Control and Prevention (CDC) had opened up a preventative medicine residency to veterinarians and dentists, and Gail encouraged one of her epidemiological intelligence service officers (EIS) to apply. "She was the first veterinarian EIS officer to get a preventative medicine residency rotation with the CDC," Gail announces proudly.

Eventually, the ideas of her earlier mentor Dr. Kram began to call her to her next post. He had come back from his AVMA Congressional Fellowship ecstatic, and that excitement had been waiting for the right time to blossom in Gail. "I think of a mentor as someone who shares his or her passion, plants some seeds, and helps open doors," she says. "Malcom did that for me." She became an AVMA Congressional Fellow in 2008–2009. It was a heady time, right when Barack Obama was elected president, and she was working on tobacco legislation and the Affordable Care Act with Senator Bernie Sanders long before his presidential bid. Among other things, she learned that she really loved being in Washington, DC.

From Minnesota to Manhattan to Seattle to Kansas, the glass offices of the Pew Charitable Trusts in the nation's capital seem like a good metaphor for this cross-country veterinarian turned epidemiologist. It allows her to see clearly the relationship between human and animal health, to link her grandmother's farm background to her day job, focusing on industrial farming and human and animal use of antibiotics and innovation. From her current vantage point as president of her eponymous consulting company, she can look back and forward with clarity.

Somehow she was able to traverse the country and reach high levels while raising two children. As with almost all women who have children, the quest for balance between work and family has been more of a work in progress than a perfect achievement. When Gail's children were younger and she'd call home to say she was leaving in a half hour, "They'd say, 'Is that half an hour real time or half an hour health department time?'" she laughs. "I did try to do some of the 'being all things for all people' with kids and others, and realized that there's not enough time in the day for that." Now that her children are grown and she has more time, she's been canning vegetables the way her grandmother did.

It was that farm girl grandmother who was her first mentor. Gail tears up telling her story. She had only gotten through the sixth grade. Her father had sexually abused her and told her that she didn't need any education. "But she told my mother and later told me that I could do anything and be anything," she remembers. "When I said I wanted to be a veterinarian in a time when girls were discouraged from science and math and told to take typing instead of biology, my grandmother and my parents totally supported me."

The first time a career changer takes the leap, it can feel like jumping off a cliff; it's more scary than exciting. But once she realizes that she's not flinging herself into the abyss and that the ground is just a few feet away, the next risk is more exhilarating. For Valerie, her changes always followed careful preparation and there was no leaping before she looked. Heather pursued opportunities wherever she could, seeking the wide world that veterinary medicine offers and pushing past comfort for change. Gail wanted to learn and serve at the juncture of human and animal health. Each of these women was willing to make changes despite their comfortable, successful lives.

All career changers recognize when it's time for something new. Whether they're feeling bored and unchallenged, looking for a new way to be involved, or want to move over and let new folks step up, leaders who change careers do more than prove that veterinary medicine is a versatile profession. They invigorate our sense of what is possible and help us consider stepping a little closer to the edge of our own next leap.

Takeaway Tips

- Seek out opportunities but also truly consider those that seem to appear out of nowhere. Sometimes when you deviate from your planned path, it turns out you're really in the right place at the right time. Be an opportunist in the best sense of the word.

- Learn how to take risks responsibly. Dr. Valerie Ragan likes to stretch, but she stretches "safely" by over preparing. That builds confidence. Know thyself.
- Treat everyone with respect, regardless of the job or the status that they were born into—whether president or gardener. The person you hire could be your boss someday. You respect the position, but more importantly you respect the person.
- Dr. Heather Case has learned to detect when she's bored and knows when it's time for a new challenge. When she's made a career switch, she's learned to be comfortable being uncomfortable for a while. Learn to recognize the feeling of stasis and heed the difference between feeling comfortable versus feeling stale. Practice being uncomfortable in new, low-risk situations until you're ready to make a bigger change.
- Like Dr. Gail Hansen, even if you're not sure you'll get the job or even want the job, consider interviewing for it. You'll clarify your goals in the process, you'll open yourself up to a new opportunity, and you just might get the job.
- Practice mentoring generosity and tell others that you believe in their ability to succeed in new positions. Dr. Heather Case learned to believe in herself when someone else showed faith in her.

Notes

1.   Katie Burns, "Taking the Leap: AVMA, Virginia-Maryland Center Among Groups Helping Veterinarians with Career Transitions," *Journal of the American Veterinary Medical Association News*, June 17, 2015, https://www.avma.org/News/JAVMANews/Pages/150701a.aspx.

2.   "Revealing the Real Millennials: Career Expectations," *Catalyst*, July 13, 2015, http://www.catalyst.org/knowledge/revealing-real-millennials-career-expectations.

3.   Helen S. Astin and Carole Leland, *Women of Influence, Women of Vision: A Cross-Generational Study of Leaders and Social Change* (San Francisco: Jossey-Bass, 1991).

4.   Stanford Distinguished Careers Institute, http://dci.stanford.edu.

5.   Judith M. Bardwick, "The Seasons of a Women's Life," in *Women's Lives: New Theory, Research and Policy*, ed. Dorothy G. McGuigan (Ann Arbor: University of Michigan, 1980), 35–37.

6.   Vivian Giang, "You Should Plan on Switching Careers Every Three Years for the Rest of Your Life," *Fast Company,* January 7, 2016, https://www .fastcompany.com/3055035/the-future-of-work/you-should-plan-on-switching -jobs-every-three-years-for-the-rest-of-your-.

7.   Ibid.

8.   Vet Partners, http://www.vetpartners.org.

9.   Claudia H. Deutch, "Behind the Exodus of Executive Women: Boredom," *New York Times*, May 1, 2005, http://www.nytimes.com/2005/05/01 /business/yourmoney/behind-the-exodus-of-executive-women-boredom.html.

5

Beyond Fake It 'Til You Make It

Anne Corrigan applied to veterinary college as a twenty-one-year-old. Her first rejection came a few months later. She applied again the next year to thirteen different veterinary programs and was again denied. To improve her chances for admission she worked in a clinical practice and secured a second bachelor's degree, this one in zoology with an emphasis in animal behavior and neurobiology. The next year Anne applied to the same thirteen schools. Again she was denied. She enrolled in a master's program in zoology, completed her degree, and applied again. In total Anne applied five times to veterinary programs before she was finally admitted in 2000.

Today when she strides into the lecture hall, twenty years after her first rejection from veterinary school, Dr. Anne Corrigan's students at St. George's University see a confident professor of small animal medicine and surgery, board-certified in veterinary internal medicine. Among the eighty-one full professors at the veterinary college, she is one of just five women with that designation. On the university's small island campus, it's routine for students to bump into their professors at open-air restaurants and on the beach. Anne has given impromptu explanations of course material in her bathing suit, her tattoos on display and flowing hair unencumbered. She's comfortable discussing, say, chronic renal failure while sitting on a beach towel, chairing a promotion and tenure committee, and lecturing to a class of a hundred, all in the same day.

Clearly a leader, she doesn't always think of herself that way. Like Anne, despite their accomplishments, many women don't consider themselves to be leaders. Leaders are *those* people, the ones up high on a pedestal—the superwoman, the alchemist who somehow creates more hours in the day to become the practice owner, head of the state association, board-certified surgeon, and full-time mother of two who helps with homework while studying for her second boards. The rest of the pack are average veterinarians, "just" practice associates or instructors—the followers.

Psychologists call the persistent feeling of being less than, of being a fake—experienced by high achievers, particularly high-achieving women—the impostor syndrome. We talked with women about their struggle to overcome not only this feeling but also their drive to be perfect, to be liked, and to avoid conflict. In this chapter Drs. Anne Corrigan, Lauren (Nicki) Wise, and Catherine (Kate) May expose their feelings of inadequacy and perfectionist tendencies to a group of St. George's University students. Dr. Ashley Harris, a medical director who oversees the New York region for Banfield Pet Hospital, reveals how her biggest professional hurdle was coming to terms with her mother's accomplishments as a medical educator. Michelle Forella, a third-year Cornell University student, shows how she succeeds at leadership as an introvert, a reformed perfectionist, and someone who has learned to "fake it 'til she makes it." University of Georgia Dean Sheila Allen talks about the desire for perfectionism that clogs the academic pipeline, while Louisiana State University Associate Dean of Diversity Lorrie Gaschen explains her impetus for launching a mentor program to help new faculty, particularly women, understand how their need to be liked can stall their professional development.

The Impostor Syndrome and Perfection Complex

The impostor syndrome—feelings of inadequacy and fraudulence even when evidence shows the opposite—is different than simply feeling new to a group. Psychologists Pauline Rose Clance and Susanne Imes popularized the concept in the 1970s within the context of their studies on high-achieving women in their article "The Impostor Phenomenon in High Achieving Women: Dynamics and Therapeutic Intervention."[1] Since their first study, gender-blind studies have shown that men and women are equally likely to feel fraudulent, and in fact 70 percent of all professionals feel like fakes at some point.[2] The person who suffers from the impostor syndrome truly feels that despite her accomplishments, she doesn't belong among the others— other students chosen to be in vet school, professors, clinical specialists, researchers . . . fill in the blank. She's sure that somebody made a mistake in her admittance, nobody else would take the job, she got lucky, or all of the above. She's just waiting for her superior to look up over his or her glasses and say, "Excuse me, we need to talk." Different than actual impostors who are masterful at reading social cues and acting the part with pitch-perfect fakery, people who experience impostor syndrome misread cues and are convinced that they'll be found out for their hidden incompetence. "Deep down, psychologists suggest, impostors appeal to us because we suspect that we are all, to some degree, faking it. Their stories expose the kaleidoscope of the self itself, and how to keep one step ahead of feeling like nobody our-selves," says Bruce Watson in the *Nautilus* article "Catch Us If You Can."[3]

A close cousin of the impostor syndrome, the perfection complex is the attitude that every paper, project, or proposal must be flawless. More than just healthy striving to do one's best, the perfection complex is a relentless drive to deliver a precise and faultless performance each and every time.[4] Perfectionists focus on their shortcomings rather than their accomplishments, compare themselves negatively to others, and experience high levels of stress. Those with a perfection complex rarely celebrate their accomplishments because they're worried about hitting the exact mark on the next challenge. The impostor syndrome and perfection complex, often intertwined, commonly afflict high-achieving people.[5]

Of deep concern in veterinary medicine is the fact that perfectionists and people who feel like impostors often have stress-related health issues.[6] Because they're usually very successful, they're hard to spot and tend to suffer alone, compounding the sense of isolation. Emotional exhaustion related to maintaining a front and fear of being found out can contribute to burn out, according to Sandeep Ravindran in "Feeling Like a Fraud:

The Impostor Phenomenon in Science Writing," in *The Open Notebook: The Stories Behind the Best Science Writing.*[7] "Professional success may not serve as an antidote, either," he writes. "In fact, it can actually exacerbate the impostor phenomenon by making people feel more exposed and more likely to be found out. That can lead to a fear of success, which causes people to actively avoid putting themselves in a position to succeed."[8] Veterinary wellness, success, and the pursuit of leadership come into sharp focus when dealing with the impostor syndrome and perfectionism.

St. George's attracts a special breed of professors, many with an adventurous and bold spirit, sometimes willing to earn less than their stateside counterparts to pursue their profession. During a faculty panel on the impostor syndrome and perfection complex, Anne acknowledges that her rise to full professorship would not have happened so quickly at a school in the United States, but that doesn't make her feel less confident. She does feel like an impostor, though, when she serves on committees as one of the few women among older men, and wonders if they'll take her seriously. "I have to tell myself that I'm an excellent member of the faculty and have the credentials to be sitting there with them," she says.

"My impostor syndrome is mixed into my perfectionism," she continues. "If I don't prepare extra hours for a meeting or a paper, the feeling that I'm going to be found out starts to creep in." She's eased up quite a bit since her earlier days, but even now she can feel overwhelmed by the sense that she's been fooling her senior colleagues. When she revealed this on the panel discussion, the students couldn't believe what they were hearing. Outside in the ninety-five-degree heat, the sun beat down and a swath of aquamarine-colored water peeked out between whitewashed buildings on campus, but inside all eyes were riveted on Anne Corrigan.

"I was quaking in my boots when I had to present research last week," she told the students, "and I was sure that the review team would know that they'd made a mistake in making me committee chair. Dr. Wise over here stuck her head in my office when I was going over my paper for the thousandth time and said, 'You got this. Come on, you'll be fine.' Her confidence boosted my own."

The students were stunned that their teacher, the woman with the quick wit who moves confidently through the lecture hall, experiences excruciating self-doubt at times. "I used to think it was just me," said one student. "Then I realized that a lot of students have it. I never realized that faculty also suffers from the impostor syndrome."

Dr. Nicki Wise, associate professor of large animal medicine and surgery, didn't think that anyone else felt like an impostor until her internship, when she finally felt comfortable bringing it up with a colleague. She was shocked and comforted when her friend confessed to having the same issues. "For the first time, I felt like I was on a team rather than on my own," she told the students.

"Actually, the perfection complex is bigger for me than feeling like an impostor," she laughed. A redhead from South Carolina whose smile punctuates her sentences, she peppers conversation with "ya'll" and adds "honey" for students who need an extra dose of warmth. Her mentor was the one who helped her break the pattern of perfectionism before it broke her.

"I went from my residency working eighty to a hundred hours a week, including nights and weekends, into a PhD program with the USDA. My major professor (greatest mentor and boss to ever live!) and I were working on an experiment, and I had been dealing with it all week," she said. He needed the results for a presentation on Monday. Nicki went to his office on Friday afternoon, head hanging, telling him they had hit another speed bump and she'd have to start over again. She insisted she would work all weekend to get it done, but he assured her that the experiment was fine, and when Nicki argued that it wasn't good enough, he sat her down.

"You can work all weekend and the sum total efforts of all your work will likely not even be noticed by the audience," he told her. "The only accomplishment of working all weekend will be for you to be tired and burnt out." The lesson was striking.

"It was important to him as my boss to see me reward myself for a week of hard work and relax rather than try to achieve some made up level of perfection that I had created," she said. "He presented that research the next week with all the pride a father would have. It really showed me that you can make time for yourself and it's okay. And more importantly, this interaction and countless others showed me what a real leader is, what a real 'boss' does—to take pride in and lift up his employees, not micromanage. His message was to care about the person and the work will fall into place."

As codirector of the Professional Attributes Workshop (PAWS) for first-year students as well as leader of a professionalism course in third year, Nicki helps students understand that perfectionism can be downright unhealthy. One student at the panel discussion chewed her pen nervously as her professors talked about a hot topic in veterinary medicine—compassion fatigue and mental health. Long considered the primary affliction from working in a caring profession, where the toll of everything from animal illness to euthanasia to supporting grieving or demanding clients, compassion fatigue and burnout is a serious problem. Many in veterinary medicine are taking a closer look at perfectionism as contributing factor of burnout, depression, and even suicide. And perfectionism and stress seem to be gender slanted toward women, according to the authors of "Gender Differences and the Definition of Success: Male and Female Veterinary Students' Career and Work Performance Expectations" in the *Journal of Veterinary Medical Education.*[9]

Dr. Kate May, another panelist, nodded. "Being a perfectionist became a health issue for me when I was younger," said the South African professor. "Ten years ago I pushed myself so hard I got sick and developed an autoimmune disease that I attribute to stress." She had to take a step back or risk getting worse. A soft-spoken woman, she was forced by her illness to reassess what's important to her. Now she says she has better balance. "Being happy and maybe not so perfect is what I aim for," she said.

The student chewing on her pen sighed. "I had to be perfect to get into vet school, and I can't imagine ever feeling like I don't have to be perfect to succeed. I want to specialize in oncology, so that means I have to work extra hard now to get an internship and residency later."

Kate looks out at students, leans forward, and urges them to avoid her mistakes. "You have to realize that not everything needs to be perfect, that it's you who's putting the impossible standards on yourself. It just has to be good enough! So cut yourself some slack and make sure that you have balance in your life and do things to make you happy. And prioritize the most important stuff that you need to get done and then do that. If you have time, you can do the other stuff. And don't say yes to everything! People will pile work on you because they know that you will push yourself to do it."

"Phew!" she laughed, leaning back.

Back in the United States, Michelle Forella, Cornell '17 can relate. In college, vet school seemed so far away, laden with endless obstacles. Perfect grades, the right work experience, tons of extracurricular experience . . . all had to be lined up and checked off. "I was an inexperienced nineteen-year-old," says the six-foot-tall former basketball player. "It all seemed overwhelming and impossible. Somehow I just took little steps that would get me one step further so I could check boxes along the way to vet school," she says. She got a job at a farm near her suburban Connecticut home, which allowed her to volunteer at a children's museum wildlife sanctuary, which in turn helped her get a job at a vet clinic. "Somewhere along the line I thought that I can do this, I *am* doing this, and then I felt prepared and I was ready to apply."

The first class was a fourteen-week course that integrates anatomy with other subjects. It is overwhelming and reputed to be the hardest course. Michelle says, "Everyone freaks out about it, and it *was* super hard." She loved it anyway and did very well, getting A's just like she did in high school and college. But vet school is notorious for knocking the wind out of perfectionists when, after a lifetime of high academic performance, they get their first B or C. "That's when we really freak out," she says.

One can imagine friends being drawn to Michelle. She's athletic and smiles easily, and she's candid about her strengths and challenges in a way that veers from confessional and lands closer to self-deprecating. At Cornell, she surrounds herself with friends who share the mentality that they don't have to get all A's.

It was in second year that they got the especially difficult classes, and she worried that it would be impossible in the four years to learn everything she needed to know in order to be responsible for the lives of animals. She and her friends supported each other going into their infectious disease course, telling each other that they didn't have to know everything but to just get through and learn what was important to know. "Perfect isn't the point, knowledge is" Michelle reminded herself. And she took baby steps to build confidence. Whether strategy or "maybe that's just my reaction when I have that fear," the process works for her and now she says she is ready to start clinics.

Out in the world after graduation, it's harder to be methodical and gradually build the skills needed for the desired job, and harder still to have that job come along when one feels ready. Dr. Sheila Allen, who graduated in the first Cornell class to have over 50 percent women, recently retired from the University of Georgia as the dean of the veterinary college. She says that her mentor pushed her beyond her own sense of readiness to take her next step. If she had waited until she felt perfectly prepared, she wouldn't have become dean.

"I got lucky because the associate dean position came along, frankly a little early in my career, and Dean Keith Prasse helped me understand that you can't wait for something to be easy or convenient," she says.

"This job isn't going to be open in two years when you think you're ready," he bluntly told her. "It's ready now, so you had better get ready. You've got the right stuff, you will grow into the job and I think you can do it."

Sheila has used her position as dean to encourage other women in the academic pipeline to move up and apply for administrative posts even when they don't feel ready, a problem that plagues qualified women in academia and propels them to "downshift" their goals and give up on becoming tenured faculty in greater numbers than their male counterparts.[10] Sometimes it takes more than encouraging words. She worked with a faculty member for months to get her to explicitly state what she would need to move into an administrative role, coaching her to negotiate for her requirements. Negotiation itself is tangled up with perfectionism for women, from salary to flexibility.[11] Sheila's breakthrough came when she helped the professor realize that she didn't have to be absolutely qualified and matched for the position but could grow into it. Sheila convinced the professor that she had the core skills and could negotiate for the time she needed to continue her research and take care of her family while handling administrative duties.

Likability

Likability is a theme that comes up repeatedly when women speak of internal barriers to success. The need to be liked motivates many to act in ways that are genuinely positive and that foster supportive relationships, but this need can also hold them back. Women are socialized to be nice, polite, and collaborative—all positive qualities—so when they strive to achieve, they can feel that some of their behaviors will make them unlikable. That's a big cultural stereotype to overcome.[12]

Harvard University researcher Deborah Tannen was one of the first to explore how even as young girls, females use language in ways that smooth differences and disagreements and reinforce collaboration.[13] When a conflict arises, girls tend to talk about it circumspectly and in ways that preserve their likability or appearance of likability.[14] It's not so much that they avoid conflict as it is that they deal with it indirectly. Women tend to avoid confrontation, which can leave issues unresolved. The skillsets used by mediators and specialists in conflict resolution, such as active listening, calm and clear communication, and commitment to mutual respect, can help women approach conflict in a way that does not feel direct or combative and is more in keeping with their gender expectations. For women whose need to be liked is a professional liability, gaining an understanding of their conflict patterns and developing conflict resolution skills helps them to become more effective leaders. Dr. Rene Carlson refers to this as "practicing positive conflict" in the chapter "For the Greater Good."

Michelle Forella is developing an awareness of conflict and likability early, and that bodes well for her future. Until recently she tended to avoid conflict in all her extracurricular groups, but she wants to get better at "dealing with all the conflict and drama." There's a difference, though, when she's assessing a new group or job. "I'm always a lot quieter in the beginning," she says. "Part of it is judging the different dynamics and figuring how to best fit in. Likability plays a part, but it's part strategy, too."

For Michelle, a simple example of this strategy is in writing emails. She's well aware of women's tendency to say "I just was wondering" or "I just wanted to say" instead of directly asking or stating something. "I try to avoid saying 'just' and to speak more directly, the way a man might," she says. She has deleted "just" from her emails, only to add it back again because she thought it would be more effective to come across as less blunt. She laughs at how much energy she puts into figuring out the best tone for an email. And when she wants to be sure she gets her point across, Michelle speaks directly, and often "the way male students do, without a second thought," she says.

Michelle has noticed how women defer to men at SAVMA (Student American Veterinary Medical Association) symposia so she does her best to be heard and seen when she's representing other students or wants a professor to know she's adept, as in a recent clinic on emergency medicine. Sometimes clinical directors make sure to call on each student because they're aware that males don't always share the air, says Michelle, but in this case she needed to speak up for herself. "Forget worrying about being liked or too nice in those situations; it's my job to speak directly," she says.

Kate May's approach to likability has also evolved. Early in her career she avoided conflict as much as possible because she wanted to be liked and had a hard time saying "no." "By taking on too much, telling myself that I can do it, and then setting myself impossibly high standards, I pushed myself hard," she says. She didn't want to rock the boat and would take on the jobs that no one wanted and work after hours or weekends. Now a little older and wiser, and committed to her own wellness, she strives for better balance.

Associate Dean Lorrie Gaschen of Louisiana State University points to the ways likability plays out for assistant professors and residents. Junior professors, new to the supervisory role and not far in age from students in the clinic, can tangle up friendliness with being friends—and sometimes more. It is possible to navigate the terrain between friend and professor, between buddy and role model, but it's extremely tricky, says Lorrie. "A lot of residents and junior faculty haven't settled into their new role as teachers and feel uncomfortable with supervising. They confuse authority with being authoritative." She sees occasional over-fraternizing that can be awkward or confusing for students and delays the path to gaining respect for residents or junior faculty—and in some cases torpedoes it all together. In response to what she sees as a lack of professional orientation and training for new residents, Lorrie is developing mentoring workshops and programs to help them develop these "softer" yet critical skills.

Beyond "Fake It 'Til You Make It"

As children we mimicked adults. Copying their behaviors helped us to learn even though we didn't understand everything they did. As young professionals, it is normal and even advantageous to observe the bosses we admire and try on their style until we develop our own.

Rather than considering "faking it" as something negative (as if the goal is to avoid being found out), we can reframe it as "following the maestros," which creates a positive connotation. Just as an apprentice potter studies with her master teacher, producing piece after piece in the teacher's style, she learns by emulating until she's skilled enough to develop her own style. Some of the strongest leaders are those who started out copying their role models, feeling fine about trying on their styles and mannerisms while utilizing the skills they were taught. In a culture that values individuality, it can be a source of shame to not feel completely original, but borrowing someone else's style can be an effective way to vault into our own identity during the early stages of learning. We might feel that we are in over our heads, but we can act the part for a *little while*—working hard, surrounding ourselves with smart and supportive people, and eventually learning what we need to do to perform the task confidently and competently.

Emulating masters is not a long-term prescription for slacking and posturing without real competence; it's a strategy for pushing oneself into professional roles that, as a perfectionist or someone who is paralyzed by lack of confidence, one would otherwise avoid. It takes a certain level of confidence to cover for perceived lack of competence, say Kattie Klay and Claire Shipman, authors of *The Confidence Code*,[15] and acting the part comes easier to those with social confidence, allowing them to try on roles while they learn skills. According to the authors, too often women underestimate their competence, and their confidence suffers, while men do the opposite.

"Fake it 'til you make it" is inappropriate in veterinary medical situations where the health of a patient is at stake. Nobody wants a veterinarian to fake competency over confidence. "Fake it 'til you make it" is a normal strategy, though, for getting through situations where confidence has not yet caught up to actual skills and competence.

In the 1970s and early 1980s, when the American College of Veterinary Surgeons was in its developmental stages and there was not today's abundance of board-certified veterinary surgeons to supervise young trainees around the clock, even in some of the most well-known academic institutions, residents—mostly male—were occasionally forced into making medico-surgical decisions on their own. When required to do increasingly complex procedures, usually during evenings or weekends when they might be in over their heads, they would gather their confidence with the phrase "See one, do one, teach one." The implication was that they had already observed the procedure and now would have to perform it themselves, with the next step instructing a more junior resident to perform the procedure. Though not necessarily ideal, it was a positive approach that did away with any negative associations of "faking it."

In the early years of clinical medicine when curricula at land-grant colleges were mostly oriented to agricultural animals and horses, veterinarians who migrated to the cities often found themselves learning about small animal medicine by consulting with physicians, learning from each other, or, most commonly, learning by the "seat of their pants."[16] A few decades later, upper-class students might return to college after a summer of looking after a single veterinarian's large animal practice more or less on their own. Practice owners, ready to leave their demanding rural practice filled with midnight emergencies and bovine dystocias at all hours for their long-awaited vacation, occasionally hired these students to run their general practice. They essentially said, "Glad you're here. Here's a map and the car keys. Try not to kill any animals. See you in a month." These young men of five decades ago, though just as frightened by the realization of their inadequacies as today's women, were able to convince themselves that they could do it because the norm was to learn "trial by fire" or "by the seat of their pants." They realized that they were the best resource available to veterinarians at the time; women today who build confidence on the job know that they are the best resource as well.

Another way to look at building confidence on the job is "stretching into a new identity." Identity stretch is part and parcel of taking on a new role, and it comes more naturally to some people than to others.

Psychologist Mark Snyder identified the psychology of "chameleons,"[17] people who are naturally able and willing to adapt to the demands of a situation without feeling like a fake. Chameleons rely on strong core selves defined by their values and goals but have no qualms about shifting shapes in pursuit of their objectives. On one hand, they're flexible about trying new styles and can adapt easily. On the other, if taken to the extreme, they're unanchored to a sense of self and can mimic the people to whom they aspire in ways that make them seem like con artists.

At the opposite end of the spectrum are people who have a very strong sense of self and are "utterly stubborn in their adherence to the sense of being right no matter what," Snyder says. "If a situation doesn't mesh with that sense, they are totally unwilling to change to fit in" and they suffer the "social costs of their rigidity" because they cannot stretch into roles that feel foreign. Snyder says that most people tend to fall somewhere in the middle and are comfortable assuming new roles.

Older But Not Always Wiser

It seems strange that the experience and wisdom that come with age would not make things easier for everyone, but it's actually harder for some people to get past their impostor feelings when they are older and already successful. When we've been successful we draw from the patterns that have worked for us in the past, but we can get stuck if we are not willing to try new techniques. As we progress through our careers, we are promoted and given more responsibilities that come with greater costs. A young intern might make a mistake, and as awful as that feels, it might be salvageable or the consequences are confined to a single case. The new practice owner's clinical mistake might harm the patient, the practice's bottom line, and an associate's financial security. When the stakes are higher, the voices telling us that we shouldn't be there can come back loud and clear, at any age.

In her *Harvard Business Review* article, "You're Never Too Experienced to Fake It 'Til You Make It," author Herminia Ibarra describes the role of learning by mimicking during the progression from novice to professional. Novices copy favorite bosses and colleagues in an effort to look as if they know what they are doing—even when they have no clue, says Ibarra. As we gain experience and become successful, we develop our own way of doing things. We become more certain about what we "know" and who we are. Copying others feels wrong, so we stick with what feels natural and authentic. According to Ibarra, that's exactly what gets us into trouble as we hit career transitions that call for new and different ways of leading.[18]

Ibarra states that people gravitate more readily to chameleon strategies earlier in their careers, when it is easier to accept and express ignorance. With experience and success, our habitual ways of thinking and doing become more entrenched and our professional identities solidify. Because we believe in being true to our natural selves, we continue to act in ways that spring from our sense of who we are—even when it becomes blatantly ineffective. The effort we put into protecting our "true" identities, says Ibarra, can really hold us back later in our careers, when we are trying to build on past successes to take on bigger roles as leaders.[19]

"When we are working at improving our game, a clear and firm sense of self is a compass," says Ibarra. "But when we are looking to change our game, a rigid understanding of authenticity is an anchor that keeps us from sailing forth. Doing what doesn't come naturally feels like a betrayal of the identity that has actually has generated success."[20]

Suppose Dr. Sally Jones, a veterinarian who has excelled because of her excellent clinical skills, is now asked to supervise interns and teach them new procedures. She delivers her lessons and supervision in the same decisive, analytical approach that has gotten her far, but her work in this role falls flat. Maybe she even alienates some of the people she's supposed to be supporting. A better way would be to look at other clinicians who seem to be connecting well with interns and helping them learn skills effectively. She could take on their style and approach, mimicking it and using their language even if it feels like she is speaking a foreign language. Eventually, as she sees herself becoming more successful as a teacher, the approach and language will become her own and she'll have grown professionally.

Introverts and Leadership

Michelle Forella has already had plenty of practice stretching into new roles. In recent years she has become an officer of the Student Chapter of the American Veterinary Medical Association (SCAVMA) and a founding officer of the first student chapter of the Women's Veterinary Leadership Development Initiative (WVLDI). For her WVLDI role, she and her colleagues won Cornell University's prestigious Cook Award for making significant contributions to improving the university climate for women. But because she considers herself "highly introverted," stretching herself takes extra effort.

As an undergraduate, Michelle was hired to work as a technician at a small animal practice, Advanced Veterinary Care in Farmington, Connecticut. She had no prior training other than working at a clinic in high school and taking some science courses. The veterinarian who hired her assured her that she would learn along the way, but Michelle felt completely out of her league—like an impostor—and she felt that her introverted nature made it worse. The vet trusted that she would learn, however, and the staff helped her while always putting the patients' care first.

One day Michelle was on the phone with a worried client who had a question about his dog, which was having seizures. Although she felt unprepared to respond, something clicked in Michelle, telling her that she needed to speak with confidence for the client's sake. "I told myself right there that they can't tell my age and that I don't know much. What they need is to be reassured about their dog," she says. "I understood then that it's not about me but about them and I need to assume this sort of persona for *their* benefit."

What Michelle learned about herself and veterinary medicine, both personal and clinical, during that summer and the many subsequent weekends she worked at the clinic over the following years prepared her for clinic rotations just as much as vet school, she says. The veterinarian who trusted her, Dr. Paul Chace, coated her at the White Coat Ceremony.

Michelle and some of her SCAVMA friends attended the North American Veterinary Conference recently, joining some 17,000 others. Heading into one of the crowded networking receptions, a friend told her that she wished she could be as good as Michelle at meeting people. Michelle was shocked because she really dreaded those gatherings, wishing she could retreat to a corner. The image her friend saw was not the image Michelle had of herself. "I realize that what people see isn't what's in my head. People I think are so fearless and confident probably have some introvert tendencies and impostor syndrome themselves! I don't feel like my genuine self in those situations so I do kind of act, but then I end up enjoying it," she says.

Michelle states that while acting or "faking it" helps her to feel more comfortable at networking events, in many other situations she sees it as her responsibility to act confidently because it will help someone else, as it did that first summer working for Dr. Chace. "It's reframing and twisting the impostor syndrome around from my problem to my responsibility," she says. "I tell myself that these interactions aren't about me, it's about what other people need."

Our culture heaps praise on the people who are magnetic, who pitch their ideas quickly and loudly and attract others with their talkativeness and ability to be "on." But best-selling author and former Wall Street lawyer Susan Cain points out in *Quiet: The Power of Introverts in a World that Can't Stop Talking*[21] that while our culture favors extroverts, introverts can and do thrive as leaders. Introverted leaders, who often jokingly refer to themselves as "introverts with good social skills," are some of the most compelling public speakers, brilliant creators, and effective leaders. They rally and rise to their demands, and they refuel by being alone or with one or two close people.

Not surprisingly, the majority of people interviewed for this book, leaders at different stages in their careers, self-identify as introverts. Whether they refer to themselves as, for example, INTJs (introversion, intuition, thinking, judgment) on the Myers-Briggs scale or simply introverts by any other measure, they say that once they accepted their introversion as a strength, they thrived as leaders. Do their introvert qualities make them better veterinarians? Do they make them better at connecting with the deeper aspects of patients' owners as well as the patients? Can they read animals and people well and utilize that insight to excel as leaders? Perhaps yes to all.

Further along than Michelle in her career is Banfield Pet Hospital's medical director for the New York region, Dr. Ashley Harris, who has crisscrossed the country working for a company that owns approximately 8 percent of all veterinary practices in the United States. Overseeing seventeen practices and with thirty-five direct reports, she calls herself an introvert.

Ashley grew up in Salt Lake City but spent a lot of time on ranches in Idaho owned by her grandparents, aunts, and uncles going back generations. Her father was a rancher and her mother was a PhD in educational psychology and a professional in medical education. From these poles of farming and human medicine, Ashley combined her parents' backgrounds to chart her own course. She knew that she didn't want to go to medical school but she loved science and animals, and not just those on the farm. Her wolf-friendly stance often got her into challenging discussions with her father's side of the family about ranchers coexisting with wolves.

As a hobby later in life, Ashley has blended her appreciation of the canine species, domesticated and wild, to serve as a veterinarian in elite dogsledding competitions around the world, including the Kuskokwim 300, the test run used by the Iditarod. A sled dog pulled from its pack to be examined would likely be calmed by Ashley's deep voice and assured demeanor. She loves the cold weather of her childhood home and prefers snow to heat. When we met, she was headed to Florida and then Arizona for work, but she was most excited about an upcoming personal trip to Norway, where she'd be serving as a sled dog veterinarian.

Ashley's work has taken her around the country, and her introverted nature has not been a barrier. In her first job in Idaho she worked for three men of three different generations and became the region's first female cattle veterinarian. While visiting male-run ranches she stepped right in and put the men to work corralling and restraining the cattle. The other men in the practice chided her for "needing extra help," but she stood up for what she was doing and said she was increasing efficiency and driving up the level of professionalism. Eventually bored with ranch work and later with emergency care, she took a job with Banfield to gain business skills so she might someday open her own practice.

Soon after starting with Banfield, Ashley was offered a medical advisor position and moved to the company headquarters in Portland, Oregon. Banfield had just been bought by Mars, transforming it from a veterinarian-started company into a megacorporation run by former Bayer executive John Payne. Mars executives brought with them the corporate enthusiasm for personality assessments and pushed their employees to know their challenges and build on their strengths, to "know thyself." Ashley's recognized skills as a "highly organized" introvert with "leadership agility" took her far. Her position changed, and she moved quickly as the company rapidly went from four hundred practices to almost twice that size. Along the way Ashley discovered that she enjoyed meeting people and creating educational materials for veterinary use in practices throughout the country, and she was soon asked to deliver educational seminars to large audiences. Educational seminars and teaching? That was her mother's specialty.

Ashley's mother was a strong and leadership-driven woman who raised her children while building a successful career. The two were close, and the daughter considered her mother a role model even though Ashley wanted to do "hard" medicine, unlike her mother, who was dean of education, responsible for faculty and staff development at Mercer University School of Medicine. Ashley's mother was happy in her job as educator of educators and called herself "Dean of Fun."

When Ashley's responsibilities at Banfield demanded more teaching, it wasn't just another learning curve. "I felt like a total impostor, like I was walking into my mom's turf," she says. At first she was petrified of public speaking. Her inward nature didn't help when she was on stage, but she managed to fake it and not reveal her nerves. Acting got her through: nobody seemed to notice her fear and she performed well. Along the way, she discovered that she actually liked medical education and, as it turned out, was pretty good at it.

But she never had a chance to share any of this with her mom. When Ashley was thirty-six her mother died. She was just sixty-three. The numerical symmetry of their ages and the intersection of their career paths made the loss all the more poignant. One of her mother's academic papers on team-based learning was published posthumously. Ashley used the paper at work to begin developing the company's educational tract and later became a contributing author and editor to the Banfield book, *Anesthesia for the Pet Practitioner.* "I never dreamed I would be into education and teaching as much as I am," she says, glad to continue her mother's legacy of improving medicine through education.

Having a healthy sense of self is good only if it doesn't hold you back. If Ashley Harris had said to herself, "I'm an introvert and public speaking is really challenging for me," fine. "Medical education is not my area, it's my mom's profession." Fine. But if she had said, "I'm an introvert so I'll avoid public speaking because it goes against my nature," or "I'm not an educator so I won't teach," then her self-knowledge would be self-limitation. Fortunately for both Ashley and the profession, it is not.

Takeaway Tips

Nearly every woman interviewed for this book said that at some point in her life she felt like an impostor or has driven herself hard while striving for perfection. Perfectionism and high achievement often go hand in hand, but carried on for too long the drive for perfection becomes a negative force. Just as Kate May developed health problems, others have passed up opportunities because they didn't come along at the perfect time, when the person felt completely ready or qualified. The impostor syndrome can strike when we're young and starting out, as it did with Michelle Forella, or later in a career, as it did with Ashley Harris. The women presented in this chapter have shown us that it's possible to persevere through feelings of doubt and emerge as successful leaders.

Back at St. George's, the panel was wrapping up and students were collecting their belongings. The young woman who worried about always having to be perfect lingered to talk with her professors. "When does it ever stop?" she asked. Good question. Perhaps it never does. But bringing it out into the open defuses the sense that we are the only one with a hidden secret. Experts agree that talking about it helps. They also offer a range of other strategies.

Author Herminia Ibarra suggests[22] that we identify two or three people whose leadership abilities we admire, then observe what they do especially well and try to adopt some of their behaviors. To be able to stretch into new roles and take on new leadership experiences, we need to imagine a future version of ourselves.

Another strategy for overcoming the impostor syndrome is to see understand that the associated feelings serve a purpose, according to psychologist Denise Cummins. Anxiety and the fear of success, of failure, and of being unmasked as a fraud are all unpleasant feelings—and in moderation they motivate us to do something.[23]

Others suggest that delving into our own particular brand of the impostor syndrome and coping mechanisms is the key to overcoming it. Valerie Young, author of *The Secret Thoughts of Successful Women: Why Capable People Suffer from the Impostor Syndrome and How to Thrive in Spite of It*[24] identifies five impostor archetypes, from the soloist who feels that she should never have to ask for help to the natural-born genius to whom all talents should come effortlessly. Those who suffer from the syndrome will recognize each of the archetypes, but most will identify closely with one. Young says that by identifying our own archetype and imagining what would happen—considering the costs to ourselves and those around us—if we never change enables us to move beyond self-limitations.

Most of the women interviewed for this chapter agreed that talking about the impostor syndrome openly and without shame is the first step to overcoming it. "I talk about it with my mentors and even more importantly my colleagues," says Nicki Wise. "I have numerous friends who are in similar positions and we chat constantly about feeling like an impostor and not completing a task 100 percent the way we want to. To help my colleagues, I make sure that I lift them up *every* chance I get! Having support and someone who understands is key!"

And don't worry about being liked by everyone, Nicki adds. "People naturally choose to work with people they like, but there's a fine line between that and hiding your true self in order to have people like you. Don't be afraid to be the bossy girl on the playground!"

Kate May reminds the student who feels burdened by being a perfectionist to "learn to love yourself, perfectionism and all. And once you love yourself, you won't push yourself so hard to be perfect, because you'll realize that it's okay not to get absolutely everything perfect all of the time."

"Sharing it makes it less of a secret or solitary problem," says Michelle Forella. "It's not this hidden thing that I have to be ashamed of, it's real. Because it's real there has to be a real solution to it."

At St. George's, students were filtering out into the sun, putting on caps and sunglasses. The mood was lighter and their conversation and worries about perfectionism and the impostor syndrome drifted out into the open air.

"I'm freaking about 'clin path' tomorrow," one said.

"Yeah, but you don't have to be perfect all the time," her friend laughed, bumping her arm.

Notes

1.   Pauline Rose Clance and Susanne Imes, "The Impostor Phenomenon in High Achieving Women: Dynamics and Therapeutic Intervention," *Psychotherapy Theory, Research and Practice* 15, no. 3 (1978): 241–47.

2.   Bruce Watson, "Catch Us If You Can: We Like Impostor Stories Because We're Afraid We're Impostors Ourselves," *Nautilus*, November 17, 2016, http://prime.nautil.us/issue/42/fakes/catch-us-if-you-can?utm_source=RSS _Feed&utm_medium=RSS&utm_campaign=RSS_Syndication.

3.   Ibid.

4.   Jessica Bacal, *Mistakes I Made at Work: 25 Influential Women Reflect on What They Got Out of Getting It Wrong* (New York: Plume, 2014).

5.   Valerie Young, *The Secret Thoughts of Successful Women: Why Capable People Suffer from the Impostor Syndrome and How to Thrive in Spite of It* (New York: Crown Business, 2011).

6.   Hal Stone and Sidra Stone, *Embracing Your Inner Critic: Turning Self-Criticism into a Creative Asset* (San Francisco: HarperOne, 1993).

7.   Sandeep Ravindran, "Feeling Like a Fraud: The Impostor Phenomenon in Science Writing," *The Open Notebook: The Stories Behind the Best Science Writing*, November 15, 2016, http://www.theopennotebook.com/2016/11/15/feeling-like -a-fraud-the-impostor-phenomenon-in-science-writing/.

8.   Ibid.

9.   Lori R. Kogan, Sherry L. McConnell, and Regina Schoenfeld-Tacher, "Gender Differences and the Definition of Success: Male and Female Veterinary Students' Career and Work Performance Expectations," *Journal of Veterinary Medical Education* 31, no. 2 (2004): 154–60, http://dx.doi.org/10.3138 /jvme.31.2.154.

10.   Ravindran, *The Open Notebook: The Stories Behind the Best Science Writing.*

11.   Linda Babcock and Sara Laschever, *Women Don't Ask: The High Cost of Avoiding Negotiation—and Positive Strategies for Change* (New York: Princeton University Press, 2003).

12.   Deborah Tannen, *You Just Don't Understand: Women and Men in Conversation* (New York: Ballantine Publishing Group, 1990).

13.   Ibid.

14.   Carol Gilligan, "In a Different Voice: Women's Conception of the Self and of Morality," *Harvard Educational Review* 47, no. 4 (1978): 481–517.

15.   Katty Kay and Claire Shipman, *The Confidence Code: The Art and Science of Self-Assurance—What Women Should Know* (New York: HarperBusiness, 2014).

16.   Donald F. Smith, "A Biography of and Interview with Joseph J. Merenda, DVM," https://ecommons.cornell.edu/bitstream/handle/1813/12877 /Merenda,%20Joseph%20J.%20'34%20BioInt.pdf?sequence=1.

17.   Daniel Goleman, "Social Chameleon May Pay Emotional Price," *New York Times,* March 12, 1985.

18.   Herminia Ibarra, "You're Never Too Old to Fake It 'Til You Make It," *Harvard Business Review*, January 8, 2015, https://hbr.org/2015/01/youre-never -too-experienced-to-fake-it-till-you-learn-it.

19.   Ibid.

20.   Ibid.

21.   Susan Cain, *Quiet: The Power of Introverts in a World that Can't Stop Talking* (New York: Broadway Books, 2013).

22.   Ibarra, *Harvard Business Review.*

23.   Denise Cummins, "Do You Feel Like an Impostor?," *Psychology Today*, October 3, 2013, https://www.psychologytoday.com/blog/good-thinking/201310 /do-you-feel-impostor.

24.   Young, *The Secret Thoughts of Successful Women*.

6

On Being Mentored

Who is your mentor? If you're under thirty, it's a routine question. Mentoring has permeated business and academia so thoroughly that it seems it has always existed. Most leaders possess confidence and a clear sense of direction, along with a healthy dose of humility, but few started out that way. Whether through relationships that have developed naturally or through formal programs, mentors help leaders at crucial crossroads of their careers and fan the sparks of nascent talents. For women whose additional responsibilities at home create career paths that alternately pause and accelerate or wind and shoot straight ahead, mentors are especially helpful in their trajectories. "My mentor in graduate school used to jest, 'When you're dean, you'll need to do this or that,'" recalls Dean of Veterinary Medicine at Iowa State University Dr. Lisa Nolan. "I had absolutely no vision myself of ever being dean, but I guess he did."

Mentors and Advocates

Unlike role models who act as a source of inspiration, mentors take an active role in the development of their junior colleagues. They don't simply share knowledge and contacts, and they don't just support from the sidelines, but instead they consistently push and pull their protégés, inspiring them to think big, take risks, overcome self-doubt, and launch into new directions. The best mentors don't just tap junior professionals who look and act like themselves, but rather they identify skills and qualities in others regardless of background or gender.

"I think of my mentoring as being somewhat selfish," said Dr. Gail Hansen, former senior officer at the Pew Charitable Trusts antibiotic resistance project and past state epidemiologist for Kansas. "Though it's not simply a matter of reflected glory, I like to think I've had something to do with what that person has achieved." Hansen has mentored others throughout her career and carries forward the ethic of support that she received from her cast of mentors: Shirley Johnston, Malcom Kram, and Russ Alexander.

A cast of mentors—ever evolving, they rotate in and out of our lives. Whether we think of them as our dream team, a tough love panel, or as Lois J. Zachary says in *The Mentor's Guide: Facilitating Effective Learning Relationships*, a personal board of directors,[1] it's important to invigorate the whole idea of the mentor-mentee relationship and view it as a dynamic process rather than just a static resource. Approaching mentoring as part of the growth process, seeing mentors as the people who help us create new possibilities and larger visions of ourselves, helps us move beyond the more fraught concern of finding the perfect mentor. The realization that there will be many mentors, a cast of mentors, throughout one's career helps reframe the mentor mania into mentor management.

Advocates take their support to the next level. Advocates scan the horizon for their protégés and speak up on their behalf when opportunities emerge. They reinforce their ideas at department meetings, push for their candidacy at board openings, and commit their own connections and reputation to the advancement of their mentees. Over a half century ago, University of Pennsylvania's Professor Charles Raker felt it was time for the New Bolton Center to include a woman intern among his staff. Impressed by a 1959 graduate of the University of Georgia, he recommended to the university's board of trustees that Dr. Olive Britt be appointed. An unprecedented move at the time, especially in the high-stakes environment of the equine elite establishment, Raker advocated for a woman in whom he had confidence. Britt's appointment was an overwhelming success, and during the next fifteen years, several other women were appointed at the New Bolton Center, all of whom developed academic careers of distinction.

Advocacy might be the gold standard of support, but the value of mentoring is well established—and expected—in most professional settings. Many veterinary companies have been out front for years with mentor programs, making it a performance expectation often tied to quantifi-able outcomes to measure success. It helps new staff to learn the culture of the organization and grow their skills quickly, building their profes-sional worth on a fast track. "Effective mentoring that is rooted in support and nurturing is good for both parties as well as for the entire business," says Senior Vice President of Corporate Affairs at Banfield Pet Hospital Marta Monetti. The principle that mentoring builds commitment to the company over the long haul[2] prevails within industry, yet the degree to which mentor programs are implemented or measured or simply exist varies widely.

Banfield, founded on the premise that effective practice management and excellent companion animal care can and should be linked as busi-ness goals, has built an active mentoring program into their operations. "We need our doctors and technicians to be successful because obviously it's good for the patients, clients, and business," explained Dr. Jeffrey Klausner, the company's former senior vice president and chief medical officer. "But it's also good for them and 'them' these days means women." Klausner asserts that Banfield's mentor programs help employees not just develop the skill set they need to be good general practitioners, something they may not have learned in college, but also what he refers to as *leader-ship agility*, the ability to flex and grow into higher management positions. Klausner understands what is and isn't offered in vet school. He served as the dean of the University of Minnesota College of Veterinary Medicine from 1999–2007.

"Mentoring helps employees to develop and, if they aspire to higher levels within the company and want to cross over into management and medical directorships, it allows them to feel supported as they take on new challenges, grow in new directions, and especially apply the lessons from mistakes into opportunities for growth," he says.

At Zoetis, a global animal health company, Dr. Christine Jenkins agrees. Dr. Jenkins, senior director of the US Veterinary Medical Services and Outcomes Research at Zoetis, says that reaching high levels "doesn't just happen because you're a naturally good leader. Corporate America invests in the training and provides opportunities, where you can actually *demonstrate* leadership."

Jenkins's career includes roles at four different corporations and one university. Mentoring has been critical in her career, and she cites corporate strategies to increase and accelerate the pipeline for women. She suggests that in order to see more women at top levels, other areas of veterinary medicine should borrow effective practices from the corporate world. "'Fast track' is the unspoken word in our industry," she says. Her own résumé charts a remarkable woman who has risen quickly at Hill's Pet Nutrition and Zoetis.

Mentors in Early Careers

If veterinarians don't have the structure of formal workplace mentor programs early in their careers, they look to their bosses for guidance in the clinic or lab. Sometimes supervisors turn out to be good matches with their younger staff, where rapport and constructive feedback characterize the relationship. Sometimes mentees aren't so fortunate, but they can still learn important skills, even if the relationship isn't positive or warm. In fact, a growing body of literature calls for keeping your mentor and your direct boss separate. While they might not call their boss a mentor in the congenial sense of the word, they can learn, for example, how to manage a practice differently. As one young veterinarian said at a workshop on mentoring, "I have no idea whether the director of the spay/neuter clinic liked me, and to be honest I was a little frightened of her, but I learned a ton, good and bad, and I'll be better because of her."

Dr. Michelle Pesce, a 2012 graduate of Cornell University, took an unconventional path to find a mentor while still in college. While taking a veterinary history course, she learned about Dr. Mitch Kornet and his deep commitment to mentoring interns and associates. She made a cold call to the Long Island veterinarian, impressed Dr. Kornet enough to land an internship, and today, despite working in another state in a busy practice, she stays in touch.

"As a student, I was not truly Dr. Kornet's 'equal,' yet he treated me as if he knew I would ultimately be," she says. Kornet's mentoring values and style have continued for Dr. Pesce, now an associate who uses them with the employers and colleagues where there are eighteen doctors—all her seniors. "It's a direct continuation of the style of mentorship I first experienced with Dr. Kornet," she observes. She passes along guidance to new graduates as they join the practice because she believes that mentoring is crucial to being an excellent practitioner in the broadest sense. "Clinicians, patients, and pet owners all stand to benefit," she says.

Mentors at All Stages

Best practices in managing the mentor relationship fall into two main categories. First, it's essential to actively and continuously build a diverse network of interesting people—not just veterinarians—from which mentors might ultimately emerge. Meeting people at professional events, volunteering in community activities, reaching out to alumni, and asking a friend of a friend for an introduction are all excellent ways to build this network. It's important to be proactive early in one's professional career, and not just rely on people assigned in college or business, but actively engage a broad scope of people into one's sphere.

The second point to managing the mentor process is grace. Building a wide network usually means asking for a conversation or meeting, or some kind of investment on the part of the other person. Expressing genuine gratitude, and doing so with a phone call or a handwritten thank-you note goes a long way in our email-saturated world, and it transcends the traditional, one-directional path from mentor to mentee.

For many younger people, the concern of not being able to provide anything in return to a mentor creates fear of reaching out. Reciprocity, the cornerstone to a mutually rewarding mentor relationship, promotes learning, giving, and receiving between both mentor and mentee. Harvard University Professor Edward Clapp calls this "omni-directional mentorship" and describes the effectiveness of this practice in educational settings and beyond.[3] The concept of "managing up" discussed in *Academic Medicine*[4] refers to the idea that the responsibilities of goal-setting and follow up, along with clear expectations, lie with the mentee. At all stages of a veterinary career, managing up helps the mentor/mentee relationship develop (and even end) at the appropriate time.

Mentors offer guidance during different periods of our lives, even as our needs change. Rather than feel awkward about closing a relationship or letting it fizzle, it's better to dignify the process with gratitude and a light touch. It might be appropriate to let the relationship naturally fade, with appropriate thanks along the way, or it might be better to mark the end with a formal "bless and release" acknowledgment.

Younger mentees have more to offer than they realize. They're flying past their mentors, perhaps older practice owners or senior major professors, in website development, Instagram, Snapchat, Tumblr, and other social media tools that have sprouted since these very words were typed. Along with knowing the language of technology, younger mentees are often multilingual. They've grown up without rigid race, gender orientation, and class barriers, and they're adept internationally; they navigate a world that looks much different than that of their mentors' early days. Their energy and inquisitiveness motivates their older colleagues and supervisors to think in new ways and explain established concepts through fresh approaches. They have a different and perhaps saner approach to work-life balance than their mentors. They have a lot more to give than they realize, and their gifts truly make the profession better. "Don't ever be afraid to let people know your strengths and what you can bring to the table," says Dr. Eva Evans, a 2012 graduate of the University of Tennessee.

The decision of when and how we begin and end one mentor relationship is as individual as each of us, but there are some rules of the road for both mentors and mentees. This is especially true for mentor relationships that haven't occurred organically but are a result of more formal expectations in academic or work environments. For example, clarity of purpose is essential when approaching a mentor. Consider the following:

What specific goal, action, or project do you need help with?

Do you expect a career mentor, or just someone to help you through a particular stage or challenging part of your work?

How do your goals align with your prospective mentor's values and the legacy that he or she wants to leave?

Why would your prospective mentor invest his or her time with you?

How often do you plan to be in contact, and how (e.g., in person, email, telephone, or Skype)?

How do you plan to clarify expectations with your mentor about time commitment, follow through, and communication?

The Role of Mentoring in Academia—
Relationships, Programs, and Changes to the Institution

In the academic setting, advisors, professors, and student peers all play a role as mentors. When fifty veterinarian students at the 2015 Student American Veterinary Medical Association (SAVMA) Symposium were asked whom among them had mentors, all hands shot up. Veterinary colleges routinely establish formal mentoring programs not just between senior and junior faculty, and students and faculty, but also between first-year and upper class students.

Because mentoring is so critical to women's advancement, why leave finding a mentor to chance or good fortune? Peer mentoring among students is ubiquitous, but formalized systems that expect or reward senior administrators for actively mentoring future leaders are insufficiently robust. Rather than rely on the pluck of ambitious women, or the generous spirit of those in the position to mentor, why not borrow the best practices from the corporate world and build mentoring into performance measures?

Data provided by Association of American Veterinary Medical Colleges (AAVMC) show that the increase in tenure-track professorial positions for women at all levels of US veterinary colleges changed only two percentage points, from 32 to 34 percent, in the five-year period from 2010 to 2015.[5] The loss of women in the pipeline of tenure-track faculty positions is especially troubling with a significant decline occurring between assistant to associate to full professor. And what about women at administrative levels? Since the early 2000s, over three-quarters of the students admitted to veterinary college have been women. These students will be the future workforce and future leaders, so shouldn't we expect that a substantial portion of our veterinary colleges be led by women?

Prior to building her career at Zoetis, Dr. Jenkins spent her early career in academia. During those years, she used to argue with her father, an academic administrator, that it "takes too long to become a dean." Dr. Jenkins states, "If we helped to enrich the academic pipeline and provide leadership experiences during the early stages of one's career, we would follow the lead of corporate America where upper level achievements come more quickly than in academia."

She adds that while she is extremely proud of her female colleagues who are deans, she believes "that to address the lack of gender balance in veterinary medicine and to help guide the profession, we need to shorten the time span. As a profession we need to work collaboratively to develop leadership curricula that are applicable to academic institutions similar to corporate cultures."

Unfortunately, the number of women appointed as deans of veterinary colleges lags well behind appointments of men. Between 2000 and 2015, only nine of the forty US dean appointments were women, and almost all of them agree that mentoring was key in their ascendance.

These women deans didn't come up in a time when mentoring programs were the norm.[6] In their early careers, they often developed organic relationships with their mentors, people whom they didn't even call mentors in most cases but thought of as supporters, advisors, faculty, and senior colleagues. Their outstanding mentors have mostly been men due to the timing of their entrance into a then male-dominated field.

Dr. Ruby Perry, dean of Tuskegee University College of Veterinary Medicine, Nursing and Allied Health, describes mentors as a circle of supporters essential to her growth and development. "My mentorship circle believes in me and encourages me to be the agent of change for which I have the capacity, desire, and interest," she says. Among her circle of mentors, primary is her mother who encouraged her to take advantage of every opportunity. Then there are the other African American veterinary deans whose willingness to share their experiences and keep in touch support Dr. Perry in ways large and small. She is especially grateful to the women veterinary deans with whom she interacted at the January 2015 deans' meeting in Naples, Florida. Dr. Perry fondly recalls the special kinship they felt while driving from Naples to Orlando to attend a follow-up conference.

Dr. Deborah Kochevar, dean of Cummings School of Veterinary Medicine at Tufts University, and Dr. Sheila Allen, dean of University of Georgia College of Veterinary Medicine, remember that trip. "It was kind of a Thelma and Louise and Louise and Louise and Louise trip," jokes Dr. Kochevar. Now that the cluster of female deans has expanded to nine in 2015, the group may need to add a van and shorten their name to the Thelma and Louise Caravan.

Dr. Joan Hendricks, dean of the School of Veterinary Medicine at the University of Pennsylvania, remembers the Thelma and Louise Caravan that January with renewed excitement. "When the deans met in Naples for their annual meeting, we senior female deans were delighted to meet two then interim women deans, Susan Tornquist and Ruby Perry," she says. "It turned out *both* had been approached to be candidates for dean, and we all encouraged them *both* to indeed throw their hats in the ring. It was very reminiscent, for me, of my own reluctant entry into the candidacy at Penn Vet. There I was in 2005, decrying the lack of female leadership and demurring when told I should be a candidate. So to Tornquist and Perry, we all said—'*do it*'! So they did and delightfully, Susan is now one of nine female deans in North America." So is Dr. Perry, who was appointed dean at her institution a mere ten days after Dr. Tornquist.

University of Guelph Dean Emeritus Dr. Elizabeth Stone offers another strong example. Preceding both Allen and Hendricks by a year or so, Stone says that mentoring was so effective for her early academic career at that she instituted a formal program when she became department chair at North Carolina State University. It proved to be quite successful and could easily be replicated elsewhere to help women into tenure-track positions.

Gender differences are real, and they play out in mentoring styles, notes Dr. Jean Sander, former dean at Oklahoma State University. "Women's styles and men's styles are very different. Would-be mentors tend to move toward those people who are like-minded when they reach out to bring others up behind them because of the comfort level," she says. "Because we have had so many men as leaders in this profession, the natural instinct would be to relate to another man who has a similar style and approach."

"There have been a few men who have stepped outside of that," explains Dr. Sander. "For me, it was Barney Easterday, my own dean while a student at the University of Wisconsin-Madison. But I don't think there are enough of these men yet. There's still a lack of understanding of how women's leadership styles are going to be successful."

Given the number of highly qualified women in the academic pipelines at our veterinary colleges, it seems reasonable to assume that the proportion of women dean appointments could increase to at least 50 percent in the next five years. While mentoring is an important part of moving women to higher levels, the lack of substantive structural change in the academy makes this less likely to happen easily. For example, at one major northeastern university, despite many years of affirmative action in recruiting women at every level, only one of four final candidates for dean in early 2016 was a woman.

We can wait for change to happen naturally. We might hope that more women consider entering the top academic and administrative pipeline. We can urge women to find great positions on their own, to sort out the family/life balance, and to rise to the top administrative levels. Or we can facilitate that change through a combination of strategic mentoring and structural modification.

Term limits for upper level administrators offer one way to institute effective structural change. Four- or five-year terms, renewable not more than once, would add a sense of order and institutional expectation. In addition to ensuring more frequent turnover in the most senior administrative offices, term limits would also allow colleges to anticipate the time when positions would be vacant, letting them prepare three or even four years in advance of the appointment. Though most dean searches are conducted over twelve to fourteen months, for example, the actual period of inviting people to become candidates is usually confined to a two-to-three-month window. Such a constraint discourages applicants who must consider major geographic and lifestyle moves and often narrows the applicant pool, especially for those with families. Colleges end up appointing interim deans from within the organization (historically, these are usually men), and these individuals often are selected for the permanent position. By extending opportunities for inquiry, recruitment, and extended visits of aspiring female administrators, colleges can boost the potential for a broader pool of both female and male candidates.

We also need to adopt job descriptions to accommodate greater flexibility for high-quality candidates with less traditional and more diverse professional portfolios. Do all of our colleges need deans who are internationally recognized researchers? Perhaps we need a less constrained concept of distinction, one that reflects the future needs of society rather than the traditional and narrowly defined practices of the twentieth-century academy.

Do all deans need to be expert fundraisers, constantly moving from local meetings with vice presidents for development to meetings a continent away with potential donors? Do we ever really assess the investment of international travel on time away from our offices and our families? Many deans are expected to spend several hours a week in group meetings with provosts and vice presidents. Is it time for deans to just say "no" to the unending reports that satisfy what some call the "bean counters" from their important work of meeting with students and faculty—and from their families? Accountability is important, but so are trust and a lighter hand on university centralization.

If and when deans return to spending more time as academic leaders, and less time as managers of centralized university units, they will occupy positions that are more attractive to a broader array of both women and men who desire a better balance of personal and professional responsibilities. The positive impact that this cultural transformation may have on students and junior faculty who aspire to meaningful leadership positions could be enormous.

Imagine five years into the future. Imagine the percentage of women deans increasing from 30 percent to 50 percent. Then imagine if the goal was realized not just across academic institutions, but through industry, government, and nonprofit veterinary organizations. We have the capacity to be proactive and to accelerate the process of getting more women into academic and other high-level positions of influence using best practices in mentoring and leadership curricula. In a professional field in which gender has changed so significantly in the last forty years, we have a unique opportunity—and perhaps even a responsibility—to stand out among other professions so that the profile of our academic leaders not only more closely reflects our demographics, but that it better adjusts to societal needs.

While structural change can surely expand leadership opportunities for women, the heart of change is often terrific mentorship. "You will only get an opportunity once," Dr. Perry's mentor, her mother, reminds us. "Don't let it pass you by."

Notes

1.   Lois J. Zachary, *The Mentor's Guide: Facilitating Effective Learning Relationships* (San Francisco: Jossey-Bass, 2011).

2.   Tammy D. Allen, Lisa M. Finkelstein, and Mark L. Poteet, *Designing Workplace Mentoring Programs: An Evidence-Based Approach* (Chichester, UK: Wiley-Blackwell, 2009).

3.   Edward P. Clapp, "Omni-Directional Mentorship: Redefining Mentorship as a Reciprocal Process of Teaching and Learning," Mentorship Conference, Albuquerque: University of New Mexico, 2011, http://scholar.harvard.edu/edwardclapp/publications/omni-directional-mentorship-redefining-mentorship-reciprocal-process.

4.   Judy T. Zerzan, Rachel Hess, Ellen Schur, Russell S. Phillips, and Nancy Rigotti, "Making the Most of Mentors: A Guide for Mentees," *Academic Medicine* 84, no. 1 (2009): 140–44, https://doi.org/10.1097/ACM.0b013e3181906e8f.

5.   Association of American Veterinary Medical Colleges, "Annual Data Report, 2015–2016," http://www.aavmc.org/data/images/research/aavmc%20data%20reports/2016%20aavmc%20public%20data%20-%20feb2516.pdf#page=9.

6.   Mary K. Doyle, *Mentoring Heroes: 52 Fabulous Women's Paths to Success and the Mentors Who Empowered Them* (Batavia, IL: 3E Press, 2000).

7

For the Greater Good

Mother Theresa embodied it. Ancient Chinese philosophy elevated it. Islam, Christianity, and Judaism exalt it. While most religions call for the powerful to serve others, to truly walk the talk of assistance and alms, servant-leadership is a philosophy that transcends particular religions. In the modern era, servant-leadership is a phrase coined in 1970 by Robert K. Greenleaf,[1] a corporate careerist turned workplace philosopher who developed the nonhierarchical theory back in 1964 when corporate America had only nascent alternative models.

Greenleaf wrote, "The servant-leader is servant first. . . . It begins with the natural feeling that one wants to serve, to serve first. Then conscious choice brings one to aspire to lead. That person is sharply different from one who is leader first, perhaps because of the need to assuage an unusual power drive or to acquire material possessions. . . . The leader-first and the servant-first are two extreme types. Between them there are shadings and blends that are part of the infinite variety of human nature."[2]

In veterinary medicine, state associations and the American Veterinary Medical Association (AVMA) are beacons for servant-leaders, attracting members to give back to the profession while developing their leadership skills. Dr. Tom Johnson, former executive director of the Iowa Veterinary Medical Association (IVMA) is a classic servant-leader who helped forge a state association that ranks as one of the top for innovation and involvement among women and younger graduates. Rather than indulge in holding more prestigious positions for himself, he helped students and professionals to step forward. "Our association recognized several years ago that we needed young people in the IVMA," he says, "and I see my role as a servant-leader to help make that happen." His lessons are presented in this chapter.

Dr. René Carlson started out in Wisconsin, rose through the ranks of her state association, and became the third female president of the AVMA. Today she is president of the World Veterinary Association (WVA). How she overcame doubt and built confidence using the teachings of a self-help guru is the subject of her story.

Two other midwesterners who lead the veterinary profession—their stories told here—also embody servant-leadership. Though Dr. Debbie Knapp is head of a major cancer program at Purdue University, she didn't aspire to the highly visible director position. She would be just as happy not being the leader, she insists. Paige Allen, also at Purdue, teaches in the veterinary technology program, one of the finest of its kind anywhere, and is also a board member of the North American Veterinary Community (NAVC) whose flagship program is an annual conference attended by over 15,000 animal health professionals. Despite these high-profile leadership positions, she asserts, "I don't do these things to be a leader. I do them because it's the right thing for the profession and it's my opportunity to give back."

Animal care has been inextricably linked to the welfare of humans under Dr. Karen Stoufer's watch in Nepal and in other international settings. Her interpretation of servant-leadership is fused strongly with her Christian faith. She believes in the integration of evangelism with Christ's commandments to help feed the hungry and empower the poor and marginalized. As a veterinarian in developing countries, this has been her guiding principle.

Finally, the story of one woman who has dedicated her career to elephant care in the United States shows how servant-leadership doesn't guarantee immunity from controversy. Dr. Linda Peddie has worked behind the scenes in Hollywood as a veterinarian to some of the biggest stars on screen, literally. Her care of Tai, who starred as Rosie in the movie *Water for Elephants*, hasn't put her in the limelight, but her stance on the use of the guide has. In elephant training, the guide is "a staff with a tapered metal hook used to cue the elephant's behavior which is then reinforced (with food, praise and social contact). In most cases, verbal commands replace physical cues over time, unless new behaviors are being taught."[3] Her passion for her charges has thrust her into the world of lobbying and legislation, where she's had to navigate the arena of animal rights advocates and animal care professionals.

Greenleaf's original conception of a servant-leader distinguished between traditional leadership that "generally involves the accumulation and exercise of power by one at the 'top of the pyramid'," and his own model that "shares power, puts the needs of others first and helps people develop and perform as highly as possible."[4] Today the Greenleaf Center for Servant Leadership offers scholarship and teaches essential servant-leader qualities, including listening and understanding; acceptance and empathy; foresight; awareness and perception; persuasion; conceptualization; self-healing; and rebuilding community.

Though servant-leadership is well-recognized in the secular community, others reach for a religious connotation, especially within the Judeo-Christian tradition that espouses the value of each individual—one of Judaism's principal affirmations in which human life is regarded as having inherent value. It would seem that some faith-based Christian humanitarian groups even draw an epistemological frame of reference to the lessons in the parable of the Good Samaritan or the action of Jesus in his washing of the disciples' feet. Whether drawn from religious teachings of humility and servitude or stemming from the secular, servant-leadership philosophy and practices have been expressed in many ways and applied in many contexts. Some of the most well-known advocates of servant-leadership include Ken Blanchard, Stephen Covey, Peter Senge, M. Scott Peck, Margaret Wheatley, Ann McGee-Cooper and Duane Trammell, Larry Spears, and Kent Keith. While the idea of being a servant-leader focuses on one person working on behalf and with others, a related field of ethical leadership looks at groups of people working to make society better. Contemplative leadership is based on mindfulness and even meditation for individuals and groups to understand the role of contemplation in the cultivation of empathy, compassion, and ethics in becoming leaders.[5] These are all off-shoots of the idea of leadership for others before self.

Dr. Debbie Knapp

Dr. Debbie Knapp, head of the Purdue Comparative Oncology Program (PCOP), started her career as one of several comparative oncologists when she finished her residency almost thirty years ago. But when Dr. Ralph Richardson, the director of the program, left Purdue in 1992, Knapp reluctantly accepted the baton. She would have preferred a different role but she says, "Somebody needed to do it, and I was passionate to advance the field of comparative oncology."

Debbie graduated from Auburn University's veterinary college in the early 1980s, planning to become a practicing small animal veterinarian. At Purdue, though, she fell in love with the branch of cancer called comparative oncology, and she began her long commitment to studying naturally occurring cancers in animals that have correlates to human cancer. By studying the biological behavior and results of treatment regimens in pets, Debbie and others could advance the science in both animals and humans. As a young clinician-scientist, she was blessed with what she describes as incredible mentoring. By the time she became board-certified and was granted her own faculty position, she knew that the very highest professional priority would be to advance the field of comparative oncology.

Within a few years, many of the people to whom she had looked up at Purdue were either retiring from the field or, like her own mentor, moving on to higher administrative positions. Debbie suddenly realized that she needed to not just focus on advancing her own work in bladder cancer, but to seek out other young people with potential, and then mentor them. Not only could she help residents develop into first-rate clinicians and target their research, she could create a body of knowledge that would make a significant impact. As an example, she points to her own research over the last twenty years in which her passion has focused intensely on understanding the biology of invasive bladder cancer in dogs as well as in humans.

The world of veterinary and human medicine is replete with clinician-scientists who advance clinical medicine as members of a team. What's different about the Knapp model is that she just happens to be the leader because she stepped forward when a new director was needed. It was her passion for the science and the program, not for a leadership position, that compelled her to take the leap. She used to be happy being a follower. She loved doing comparative oncology when Dr. Richardson was in charge of the program. But when he left, she got the technicians and residents together and said to them, "OK, Ralph is gone, but we still have an important job, so let's see what we need to do to keep moving the program forward." She wanted to work behind the scenes and not be the one with the director title and all the inherent responsibilities, so for two years she and another individual shared that role as partners. Then he went on to other things and Knapp became the director.

That's the key for leaders who work for the "greater good." Their mission is larger than themselves, and they're anxious to fit any role where they would do the most good to advance the cause even as reluctant leaders at first. In some cases—and that is what happened to Debbie—these leaders eventually find that they *need* to do it themselves. They find that they are good at organizing, at sharing, at empowering, and at mentoring, and that they become energized by the expansion of the circle of other investigators and clinicians with whom they collaborate.

Debbie and her sister, who works at a senior level at the Environmental Protection Agency, say that they share the functional extravert characteristic and both rise to situations when it's required of them. To advance her understanding of bladder cancer, Debbie needed to find out how oncologists dealt with some of their vexing issues, so she donned a cloak of confidence, read all she could about the subject, and "was brave enough to reach out to the medical school," she says. She developed relationships with medical professionals by seeking help without a façade, not pretending to be a peer in knowledge at that point.

The comparative oncology program, which has over a dozen investigators, clinical scholars, and technical staff, has become so highly regarded under Debbie's leadership that Rodney Page who directs the world-renowned Flint Animal Cancer Center at Colorado State University says of her, "She is a great example of leadership, mentorship and academic success. The program she directs represents one of the best examples of how comparative cancer research can create value for all species."[6]

From our vantage point, *that* is the power of servant-leadership, mature and finely tuned.

Paige Allen, Registered Veterinary Technician

In a different part of the Purdue veterinary medical complex, Paige Allen meets with a group of young women aspiring to become veterinary techni-cians. When they graduate at twenty-one or twenty-two years old, they're not thinking about cost of living or work-life balance, and, more impor-tantly, they don't think of themselves as valued members of the veterinary health care team. A straight shooter by her own admission, Paige just says it like it is and has bigger goals for them. "There's a whole world out there," she tells them, "and all you have to do is step out and grab it."

Paige's goal is to help the young women stop seeing themselves at the bottom of the totem pole. "I talk to them about building their relationship with the veterinarian, educating them on how they can free up the doctor's time, and generate a new income stream for the practice," she says. But she also acknowledges she's not sure that these young women really understand this any more than was evident to her at their age.

Raised in the Dakotas and Nevada with supportive parents, Paige had wanted to be a veterinarian from a very young age. "We even had a neigh-bor who had a vet license plate that said 'VET,' but I didn't connect the whole thing of a *vet of a foreign war* with being a veterinarian," she laughs.

Becoming a veterinarian wasn't going to happen for Paige, however. She acknowledges that she made some poor choices as an eighteen-year-old away from home, and these choices affected her grades. Though her GPA wasn't bad, her advisor said there was no way she was going to get into veterinary college. "I was really bummed out," she recalls.

Paige went home for the summer and received a flyer in the mail about becoming an animal health technician. She had never heard the term before and had to look up what it meant. She liked what she read, pursued the education in Rapid City, South Dakota, and joined a mixed animal private practice in Nebraska for two years. Eventually, though, she got bored. "That's a theme of my career," she says. "When I get bored for lack of intellectual challenge, I want to move on to something else."

Paige was fortunate to get a position at Purdue University, where she worked in the large animal clinic of the teaching hospital and later in the surgical section where she became technically proficient, especially in advanced anesthesia techniques. After several internal promotions with greater responsibilities, Paige was tapped by Dr. Pete Bill to develop a distance-learning program for the veterinary technology program. Though she had taught on the clinical floor, she wasn't sure if online education would work, but she says, "Dr. Bill was an amazing person and a great mentor."

The program she developed provided for the knowledge and analytical components of the online course to be taught didactically and the manual skills like intravenous catheterization to be taught in clinical practices. Paige also completed a master's degree in educational technology, learning approaches that go along with teaching. In 2014, the program has continued to grow and expand under the supervision of Dr. Tina Tran, who recognized Paige's potential and challenged her to even greater leadership.

When she teaches students online or on the Purdue campus, Paige infuses her worldly perspective into the lessons. With the eye of a mentor and gentle hand of an advisor, she sees special opportunities for the young women and encourages them to think big. "The hard part of this message," she says, "is that when the students are in the Veterinary Teaching Hospital, it's not well modeled for them. They are really at the bottom of the totem pole and basically do what they are told by others. So how do we expect them to be proactive with the DVM when they're graduated and working in a private practice?" She encourages them to build their relationship with the practice veterinarian so they can share what they are truly capable of doing and demonstrate how it can free up the doctor's professional time. The economic impact of a strong technician can generate a new income stream for the practice, which can potentially raise the compensation of all members of the team."

As a servant-leader whose primary mission is to advance the profession by maximally deploying the resources at hand—human and otherwise—Paige draws heavily from her life's journey and her quest for community service. The Midwest is the perfect place to blend her professional and service commitment. She and her husband started a community garden at their church a few years ago, providing fresh vegetables to anyone who wanted to come and harvest. They also used the fresh vegetables to supplement their community's mobile food pantry. When they expanded the program by purchasing a forty-acre plot of land, Paige was struck by what she called the "connected" feeling shared by a farmer's love of the land and a veterinary professional's love of all creatures, large and small. "There's a sacred communion that occurs—a respect that transcends the never-ending, sometimes heartbreaking work and extraordinary needs of the living plants and animals we choose to nurture," she says. She wonders if there something in our nature that yearns to serve, or something in the nature of our profession that calls our name. She wonders if it is some sort of "harmonic convergence" of both that brings us to the decision to commit to caring, whether it's tending to the farm, to animals, or to the people whose lives we hope to enrich. "The answer," she concludes, "is always love. We do it for love."

Paige joined the board of the prestigious NAVC in 2015. One of only two veterinary technicians serving in the position at any one time, she works side-by-side with some of the most forward-thinking veterinarians in the country. Still, she struggles with the idea that she is a leader, and insists that she just steps up when nobody else will and she has something to offer. "You don't have to have the leadership tag to be a leader in your practice," she says. "You don't have to even be the lead tech. It's about doing the right things and making the right decisions aligned with whatever moral compass you use. Do the right thing for the patient and the owner." To the vet techs she says, "You can be a leader in a team of techs, but the receptionist can also be a leader, the kennel person . . . leadership is embodied by one's manners and how one acts and how one reacts."

From Paige's nearly thirty-year career, she urges her students to remember two things above all. "First, learning is a daily activity, and second, the best way to revitalize ourselves and help our clients is to grow our knowledge and expertise," she says. Personally and professionally, we must continuously challenge ourselves and never lose the will to discover.

Dr. René Carlson

Dr. René Carlson, the third woman to hold the office of AVMA president (2011–2012), has never turned down an invitation to run for an office. But she didn't start out that way; in fact, she hit a wall early in her career. Had it not been for a radio ad that changed her life, she might never have gone beyond her small animal practice in Wisconsin to national and international service.

The turning point came after graduation, early in her marriage, when the young veterinarian felt stressed and worried about everything: her health, money, marriage, dying—everything. During that period in her life she heard the radio pitch for a course based on the work of the self-help guru of the 1930s, Dale Carnegie. She signed up for the "stop worrying and start living" course and soon became transformed, later even teaching the course.

Some of the language of Carnegie's work, such as "Public Speaking and Influencing Men in Business," could seem archaic for women, but that didn't matter. The coursework changed her. At the time she was involved in the Wisconsin Veterinary Medical Association, and for her speaking assignment one week she needed to tell a story to the class about saying "yes." She had originally said "no" to running for office for the state association, but she needed to say yes for her story assignment.

In Wisconsin, the "yes" put her up for election against a very popular veterinarian because the state association's bylaws required that two candidates run for president-elect. At the time, very few women had run for president and none had won. "I was put up as a sacrificial lamb, but I didn't even know that. I just went for it," she says with her trademark laugh. Today she laughs freely and tells stories to make a point, just as Carnegie taught. Back then, with a boots-on-the-ground approach rather than operating through a closed network, she ran her campaign, taking a picture of herself, putting it on a postcard, and mailing it to every member in the state. It wasn't a conventional approach, but she thought that's what she was supposed to do. It worked; she won.

René has never lost an election. Her openness and vulnerability are perhaps natural strengths, and her well-honed communication skills and confidence that she learned from the Dale Carnegie model has helped her to "win friends and influence people," in her case, for the greater good of the profession. What's certain is that her passion and confidence has its roots in the Midwest where she first doubted herself and finally learned to start living—living to help herself and to serve the people and animals in veterinary medicine.

When the state association executive director called René to tell her she'd won, she was terrified. "After the convention where they made the announcement, I later went to the bedroom of the friend who I was staying with, shut the door, and fell apart," she says. The battle of the election was over and now the reality of having to fulfill the high expectations hit her. "Now what am I going to do? Oh my gosh, the expectations," she remembers thinking.

Her father counseled her through her doubts and gave her a second turning point: the understanding that she didn't have to be born a natural leader but could build skills and a sense of being qualified along the way. That lesson still holds true. In 2014, when elected president of the World Veterinary Association—its first woman—she went through the same doubts, but she rallied. "I'm growing into the enormous expectations and the first six months have been a process for me," she confesses, "even at this level after all these years."

As someone who has blended personal goals with service, René's path has been unconventional. In Wisconsin, she never served on the board before her sudden election as president. She has been successful in four major national elections without taking the normal route—from AVMA House of Delegates (HOD) in 1996, to the AVMA vice presidency (2004), the AVMA Council on Education (2006), and becoming AVMA president in 2011. When she was invited to run for the World Veterinary Association presidency in 2014, she thought that she couldn't say no even though she was up against the heir to the throne. "He was from Canada, our best friend," she recounts. But she went for it, as usual.

René believes strongly that if people want to serve, they should go for whichever positions they consider right for them. The idea that one has to take an incremental path to the top, following the expected steps, is something she dismisses. "I think that the six-year commitment at the AVMA Board of Directors turns off many women, especially busy women," she said. "My advice to other women is to just go for it and don't pay attention to the conventional path of putting in years on committees, kissing the ring, paying dues. I don't think that's necessary and that's not how I did it."

For René, starting at her local association was important because it helped build confidence by getting to know people and practicing the Carnegie storytelling techniques and honing communication skills. Eventually, she became president of her local association because members take their turn in officer roles. For her that opened the door to the state level, committees, and the AVMA—hopping up rungs of the ladder rather than climbing step by step.

Through all the leadership roles she's held, René believes that there are three essential ingredients to becoming a good servant-leader: public speaking, advocacy, and media relations. As vice president of the AVMA, she encouraged students to wade into the uncomfortable arena of public speaking and get good at it. She still tells students to take courses in it, learn to tell stories to brighten the message, and hone their message as an advocate for their passion, which is critical to success, and be concise.

"Do you care passionately about animal welfare?" she asks rhetorically. "Learn to say it in two sentences. Finally, deliver your message to the media and through social media in ways that are engaging and succinct."

René is also candid about the differences for women as servant-leaders. There will always be conflict and disagreement within groups, and it's essential to practice positive conflict management rather than avoid it altogether. Like so many women, it was hard at first for René to be disliked or to think she was. "I don't know if it's across genders, but I think that women want approval, which goes to our experiences growing up and society. I know I needed approval," she says. She has learned to express opposing views with confidence and separate the person from the opinion.

Reflecting on the role of women in organized veterinary medicine, the prevailing attitude when she was elected to the HOD was that women would naturally move into leadership positions because of the sheer numbers of women entering the profession; however, she saw that women can get stuck from moving forward, because that depends a lot on who they know and who recommends them for a position. "We aren't part of that old guard," she says. "The guys don't hang out with the younger women so they don't think of them to recommend, unless they see a rising star and want to latch on to her. That's just politics."

René has shown that leadership for the greater good and leadership for personal success aren't necessarily mutually exclusive. Her well-honed communication skills and confidence that she learned way back when in the Carnegie model has helped her win friends and influence people—for the greater good of the profession.

Dr. Tom Johnson

"We are often among the best-educated professionals in our communities," says Dr. Tom Johnson in Iowa, "so it is important that we serve in organized veterinary medicine, as well as in our local communities as civic, public health, or church officers. As educated professionals, we have an obligation to contribute to the welfare and betterment of society." Polite, direct, and all-American-looking, Tom could as easily pose for a Normal Rockwell portrait as serve as head of the Iowa State University Veterinary Medical Center. In his previous position as executive director Iowa Veterinary Medical Association (IVMA), his servant-leadership ethic infused the entire state association.

If an organization, not a person, can promote servant-leadership with a special emphasis on women, one of the leaders of the pack is the IVMA. Despite the fact that 70 percent of Iowa State University (ISU) graduates reside outside the state, almost 1,150 of the 1,450 veterinarians in Iowa are graduates of the state university. Because of this, the veterinary association and the college in Ames have always enjoyed a close and synergistic relationship.

One second-year student says, "It is all about knowing yourself and where you can best make a difference for your community." A third-year student adds, "It means leading in whatever area you are, initiating the work in your area. I think of leadership in a very broad sense. It is first and foremost giving back to the community. In the context of the state VMA, it means giving back." Students learn this philosophy on campus and through IVMA's summer internship program for those who have finished their second year of veterinary college. "By getting students involved," says Tom, "they get to know the association and its leaders, and they not only develop their own skills and commitment, but they go back to the university and influence their classmates to also consider the benefits of working in organized veterinary medicine.

Tom, a 1971 graduate of ISU, says this leadership profile didn't just happen. The IVMA had been working for over a decade, often in conjunction with ISU, to develop leadership skills and opportunities for women and for younger veterinarians. To promote young leaders and women, Tom and the association developed a two-pronged strategy. One was to make substantive structural changes in the IVMA, and the other was to develop leadership training opportunities for young veterinarians.

Structurally, they confront the prevailing dogma, just as René Carlson does, that leadership requires progressively more challenging appointments, moving sequentially from regional leadership to becoming one of the twenty-two IVMA directors, to one of the four officers, to AVMA HOD alternates and then delegates. Instead, their leaders for director, officer, and HOD positions are drawn from parallel pools of candidates so they don't have to move from one pool of qualified candidates to the next, and so on. Though there are no term limits for the directors who represent the state's geographic regions, the officer positions are limited to one year each, and the HOD members have four-year terms as both alternate and delegate. This opens up further opportunities for more members.

Officers are not usually drawn from the pool of directors who have had leadership experience in the association, so IVMA created a period of formal training and mentoring in order to develop future leaders. The development of parallel leadership opportunities widens the pool for leadership within the state. This better accommodates those veterinarians who, for either personal or financial reasons, have only so many years to give organized veterinary medicine, yet they have much to offer and are willing and eager to participate. Tom estimates the average practitioner sacrifices $1,500 of practice income for every day spent in association activities. The IVMA helps by paying travel and related expenses to encourage young veterinarians to participate in the Power of 10 Leadership Program, attend a regional leadership program, and attend the AVMA Veterinary Leadership Conference.

The results of these efforts put Iowa in the lead among state associations; women have held over 50 percent of these top positions for multiple years. Women broke into leadership in 2002 when the IVMA elected its first woman president. That was the first year Tom was executive director of the association. When asked if Iowa's structural changes and leadership development programs might be applicable at the national level for senior AVMA leadership positions, Tom's reaction was pure simplicity: "Why not?"

Dr. Karen Stoufer

Though he espouses to have little in common with people of faith, especially evangelical Christians or conservative Roman Catholics, the *New York Times* op-ed contributor Nicholas Kristof has written extensively in recent years on the impact that faith-based programs have had in remote parts of the world.[7] He is especially impressed with programs like World Vision, currently led by Cornell- and Wharton-educated Richard Stearns, which he says represent the "new internationalists, pushing successfully for new American programs against AIDS and malaria, and doing superb work on issues from human trafficking in India to mass rape in Congo."[8]

In a 2015 op-ed, Kristoff featured the work of Dr. Stephen Foster,[9] a missionary surgeon who for thirty-seven years has run a hospital, serving people with health and surgical needs in a remote area of Angola. In the world of veterinary medicine, the Christian Veterinary Mission (CVM) and its hundreds of short- and long-term "mission vets" around the world are involved in faith-based ministries involving veterinary medicine. "The thrust of CVM is all about relationships," says Dr. Karen Stoufer, who spent thirteen years in Nepal with her husband, Ron, before returning to the United States as director of training and Asia regional director for CVM.

For Karen, the concept of servant-leader was modeled by an early Kansas State veterinarian Dr. Phyllis Larson. When Karen was in high school and part of a Girl Scout program, Dr. Larson would meet with her and a group of friends on Saturday afternoons and talk about veterinary medicine. It was a selfless way for one of the early women veterinarians to be a role model in her profession. In doing so, Larson demonstrated that these aspiring girls could not only become veterinarians, but also do large animal work. When Karen, who would apply for veterinary college in the mid-1970s, was told that women couldn't be veterinarians or in particular large animal veterinarians, Karen just assumed they were ignorant. "Phyllis didn't have to tell me women could be large animal veterinarians," she says. "She showed me we could."

Years later, when Karen was helping men and women in Nepal learn to treat their animals, she knew that the day would come when she would no longer be with them in person, so she worked *alongside* them rather than *for* them. She focused on helping farmers and other animal owners learn the skills themselves so they could pass their knowledge on to others. Her brand of servant-leadership was infused with the role model mentality and "teach the teacher" philosophy; along with the technical skills, the hope was that her Nepalese colleagues would also pass along the showing rather than doing approach.

When she graduated from Cornell in 1978, Karen entered small animal practice in Snyder, New York, and later in northern California. But late in 1989, she received a life-changing call from CVM's founder and by July 1990, she settled in Nepal with her hydrogeologist husband and two daughters, then just two and five years old, to start a thirteen-year investment in one of the neediest countries of the world.

A devout Christian, Karen considers her life's work to be all about relationships. In alignment with CVM's vision of "sharing Christ's love through veterinary medicine," she says, "my relationship with Jesus Christ compels us to love and serve others, and I choose to live out my faith through using my professional talents as a veterinarian to serve others." While in developed countries, the loss of a cow may have some economic consequences, she asserts that in Nepal, it may be the difference in a child's survival or her education.

Following six months of intense language training in Kathmandu, Karen and her family headed to the rural areas to work alongside local villagers who were designated as animal health workers. These people already had many of the innate skills of animal health care, because they knew their stock and what to look for if they weren't well, "but they just didn't know what to call a disease or how to care for sick animals," she says. Within two weeks of working alongside them, they could learn how to read the numbers on the thermometer, treat a water buffalo dystocia, avoid using antibiotics unless the cow has a fever, deworm their livestock, perform wound care, and carry out rabies prevention—all of which would have a major health impact in the village. They used this knowledge to help others learn.

After four years in these communities, including working in some of the poorest villages in the country, she left the area in the hands the local Nepalese whom she had trained. She and the family moved to a very remote area in the Okhaldhunga District where they settled in a village several days walk from the nearest road. Some of the more isolated villages where she worked were a three-day walk from her own. For the next four years, her community work focused on women, encouraging them to find ways to break out of the cycle of poverty and despair. Groups of women and men received training in vegetable gardening, animal health, sanitation, water potability, and literacy. Karen and her team worked with the women as they applied for and then raised animals through a grant from Heifer International.

As Karen and her family lived and worked in the communities, they treated all people equally, despite their established caste designation. Over time, the local women saw the values of dignity and fairness that the Stoufers modeled, and they began to adopt some of these values over the traditional caste segregation. In one example, one of the lower caste women on Karen's staff was traveling overnight during a multi-day trip to another village. The staff stopped at a lodge for the evening and the owner stipulated that the lower caste woman sleep outside, which was the custom. Despite their higher caste privilege of being allowed to spend the night inside the safety and relative comfort of the lodge, the other staff chose to sleep outside with her.

Traditional societies have some practices that affect women harshly. "When you marry," Karen says, "by tradition you move into your husband's village and work for your in-laws." One woman, Lila, a mother of two young boys, married and moved in with her husband's family. Lila's husband subsequently left his wife for another woman, even taking the boys and leaving her as a slave to the in-laws. They were incredibly cruel, making her sleep in the outdoor shed with the buffalo and beg for her food while still requiring her to work for them on the farm.

Lila came to one of the women's group presentations that Karen and her staff were having on women's rights—the right to food, shelter, health. "We had a lawyer there to provide a legal basis for the group, and she said that according to Nepalese law, the children belong to the mother to the age of five," Karen says. When Lila discovered that she had a right to her sons, she decided to confront her former husband. Though she didn't have the nerve to ask for custody, she did request a tiny plot of land where she could grow her own food. Once he heard this request, the former husband became so enraged that that he beat Lila unconscious with a bamboo pole.

When Karen got the news, she felt terrible because Lila's assertiveness was the direct result of the workshop, and she wondered if this was the cost of working for women's empowerment in a culture not her own. The village women who had also been similarly informed of their rights were so upset that they forced the man to take his wife to the hospital for treatment. They assured Karen that if it had not been for workshop, the other women would not have gotten involved. "We just thought that a husband had the right to beat or even kill his wife," they told her. Until learning about their rights, "We would never have intervened."

Then the women confronted the all-male village leadership, and they in turn pressured the in-laws to build a one-room place for Lila to live and give her a piece of land for food. Lila eventually got her children back as well. "Though I questioned whether I should hold workshops like these," Karen remarks, "I realized that the impact on the other women of the village who were willing to step up on behalf of their neighbor was an important lesson in servant-leadership."

Karen says that women's empowerment is not women's work; it's for everybody. She recognizes that when women are empowered, children are healthier, and boys and girls both go to school. Boys who have educated mothers want an educated wife in the future and will treat her differently because they have seen that model. Karen's husband worked with her in women's empowerment, showing men and women both that respect for women is a strength.

By her tenth year in Nepal, Karen moved into a leadership and management role in that country, and she later returned to the United States where she works in the Seattle office of CVM. Though she is no longer directly involved with educating rural famers or facilitating women's empowerment, she is now training others in servant-leadership, using the same community development principles she practiced for over a decade on the ground in Nepal.

Her two daughters learned about being in the minority firsthand while living in a developing country. Their difference in religion, nationality, and skin color were formative experiences, and today they are committed to seeking justice for the poor. One went to law school and one is a physician. "It made them better global citizens," Karen attests, so when they hear news now anywhere in the world, they can identify with them. "From their perspectives, both refugees and the local poor look like the poor farmers in Nepal who were our neighbors and friends."

Dr. Linda Peddie

When the movie *Water for Elephants* opened in April 2011, all eyes were on Tai, the forty-two-year-old Asian elephant who played the lead role of "Rosie." Veterinarian Dr. Linda Peddie considers Tai the best-trained and most engaged elephant in the world. Linda and her husband, Dr. James Peddie, have jointly managed the health care of Tai and her herd mates at the Johnson ranch, Have Trunk Will Travel, since the early 1990s.

The array of medical and surgical challenges, as well as the sheer size and complexity of their six elephants, require extensive medical knowledge, creativity, perseverance, and a gentle touch. Tai is in extremely good health thanks in large part to the veterinary care under Linda and Jim. The Peddies are so fastidious in their care for her that during the creation of the Disney movie *Operation Dumbo Drop* in 1994, they even arranged for a 747 jumbo jet to airlift her favorite southern California oat hay to the set in Thailand.

Though Linda and Jim are regular visitors to the Johnson ranch and have examined and treated Tai and her herd mates numerous times, that familiarity does not allow them casual access to the elephants. The Peddies would never approach Tai without being accompanied by one of the ranch trainers. "Elephants form a matriarchal society," explains Linda, "and in Tai's case, Gary Johnson is the head matriarch. A trusted trainer must always facilitate interaction with a non-herd member such as one of us." Linda explained how actress Reese Witherspoon was viewed by Tai. "Reese and the others are simply props for 'Rosie,' who actually views herself as the lead actress," she says. "As long as the human stars know their place in the pachyderm pecking order, everything proceeds smoothly."

In the scenes depicting cruelty to Tai, the Johnsons were absolutely adamant that nothing harm the elephant, either emotionally or physically. A violent scene in the movie shows the trainer in the story, August Rosenbluth, going on a rampage, treating the elephant brutally. What the film doesn't show is the handlers who gently moved Tai backward and out of harm's way, leaving August to simply strike the air next to her body. "Because Tai has never known mistreatment," Linda said, "she does not view the flailing as anything more than some imbecile beating the air." In a similar manner, the ugly traumatic wounds that the movie depicts on Rosie are just convincingly fashioned latex molds perfectly affixed to her flawless hide.

Creating a movie of this nature requires a unique blend of almost mystical proportions. To more fully appreciate these qualities requires an understanding of the longstanding bonds that form between animals and humans working with mutual respect at every level. The emergence of this passionate and gifted veterinarian didn't just happen. She arose in the days when it took tenacity and courage to become a female veterinarian. Gifted with an unusual intellect, Linda was encouraged by her high school mentors to become a physician, a mathematician, a classicist—anything but a veterinarian, because that field was considered closed to women in the early 1960s.

But Linda persisted, and during spring 1961, she sat with seven other women awaiting her interview at Cornell after all the male slots had been filled. She is tall, elegant, and graceful, and today bears her decades of veterinary medicine, motherhood, and grand-motherhood with grace and dignity; however, she remembers very well the long and grueling meeting with the admissions committee several decades ago. "It was on the order of the Grand Inquisition," she recalls. "There were men seated all the way around a large table with pens and tablets ready, but they hardly looked at me." The chairman of the committee began by asking her if she cooked, if she sewed, if she enjoyed dancing, if she dated. Then he burrowed deeper: "If you were to marry someone who had a vocation out in the desert where there really weren't any animals, just what would you do with this veterinary degree?" That question really threw her because she thought, "Oh, my goodness, this man knows I'm dating a fellow from Dartmouth who happens to be studying oceanography."

Linda not only was selected as the only woman in the class that had fifty-nine men, but she graduated at the top of her class. She married classmate Jim Peddie, and they moved to California where they became partners with a progressive group of veterinarians who handled all species and managed both a hospital and ambulatory service. In addition to domestic animal practice, Linda and Jim were veterinarians to all kinds of animals, including primates and large cats, and have treated other animal stars besides the Johnson ranch's elephants. For over fifteen years, they cared for the animals in television series, such as *Frazier* and *Full House*, and in such feature films as *Dancing with Wolves*. At the height of their career, they had penetrated the inner circle of Hollywood and were working for all of the major studios. Over time, Linda and Jim also developed a close and abiding friendship with the Johnsons, and became especially knowledgeable and passionate about the beloved elephants.

While Jim often takes the more public role in working with the physical aspects of veterinary care, Linda has become particularly adept at dealing with regulatory and quarantine issues associated with moving animals between the United States and foreign countries. For many years, she was a member of the National Tuberculosis Working Group for Zoo and Wildlife Species, formatting protocols for the diagnosis and treatment of tuberculosis in elephants. She was also instrumental in establishing AVMA's policy that advocated for the use of the guide and tethers in managing elephants. This policy has helped halt legislation proposed by animal activists to outlaw use of the guide and tethers, tools she considers absolutely essential to assure the safety of both veterinarians and the elephants entrusted to their care.

Linda's passion for the continued availability of these magnificent animals to interact with children for rides and other events is deeply personal. "I feel they should be available to our children and grandchildren, and not be governed by unnecessary rules and restrictions developed by people who are uninformed and prey on emotions and falsehoods," she says. The most egregious example of such practices erupted in 2015 with the emergence of a bill (CA SB 716) that would outlaw the use of the guide in managing elephants. This law, if enacted, would either put the Johnsons out of business and force them to give up their precious elephant family to a life of misery without active stimulation or access to health care, or move them to another state with a more enlightened regulatory climate.

The impact of the law and the threats of the animal rights activists, both physically and emotionally, was particularly challenging for Kari Johnson. "Linda was so special to me," Kari says. "She helped me through the stress of last year when I had knee replacement during the period of review of CA SB 716." Kari says of the quintessential servant-leader, "Linda gives so much. I have to keep going because I can't just do less when she is doing so much. In her quiet way, she makes it happen."

In one now famous interaction during a hearing in Sacramento, Linda sat apart from the table that was lined by legislators and those testifying regarding the bill. When called upon by a legislator to testify, there was no room at the table, but she found an appropriate chair and created a dignified presence. She spoke from the heart and directly to the audience, then returned to her seat in the audience. After others had testified—many of them high-ranking with strident statements—it was she who was called back to answer additional questions. During the exchange, the legislator asked her if she was a veterinarian. According to one observer at the hearing, "Linda stood up straight and proclaimed not to be just a veterinarian, but to have been the only woman in the class of 1965 at Cornell University, and to have graduated at the top of her class."

It's easy to say that Linda works a room like no one else, but that's missing the point. She's not motivated by ego, never trying to play "gotcha," and she speaks of facts, so people are not offended. Though brutally truthful, Linda is never hurtful. She has said things to people, including those in authority, that no one else could get away with saying—"they would cause a war," Kari says—but Linda says what she feels needs to be said without ruffling feathers. Whether working the room at a legislative hearing or examining the oral cavity of an elephant, Linda uses her influence to make things better for others.

Takeaway Tips

Some people have developed organizational structures to enhance the leadership of others, like Tom Johnson at the IVMA. Others like Karen Stoufer are guided by their deep faith. Whatever the inspiration or passion, from oncology to veterinary technology, servant-leaders walk among us a little differently than others. They're leaders, absolutely, but for the greater good, and for that all of us in veterinary medicine and beyond are better off.

- You don't have to take every step on the ladder on the way to top positions. Like Dr. René Carlson, you can skip over some steps in organized veterinary medicine. Additionally, hone your public speaking skills, which are essential to your success, through good storytelling techniques.
- Consider yourself a leader in areas outside of veterinary medicine. In your community, you'll be seen as a leader. Just as Dr. Tom Johnson recommends, take on those community leadership roles and give back.
- Use your professional knowledge to get involved politically and make an impact on animal or environmental issues like Dr. Linda Peddie. Speak up, strongly and respectfully, on controversial issues.
- You can make a stronger impact if you develop a professional focus in something you're truly passionate about. Just as Dr. Debbie Knapp zeroed in on oncology, focus early on rather than dipping into many different areas.
- Consider yourself an essential part of the veterinary team, whether you're a veterinary technician or a doctor. Everyone is needed to support the patients and the clients. Leaders like Paige Allen transcend rank and title.

- Work alongside people, not just for them. Like Dr. Karen Stoufer, teach skills and service so that the principles of servant-leadership will continue when you're gone.

Notes

1. Robert K. Greenleaf, *Servant Leadership* (Mahwah, NJ: Paulist Press, 1977).
2. Robert K. Greenleaf Center for Servant Leadership, https://www .greenleaf.org
3. American Veterinary Medical Association, Welfare Implications of Elephant Training, https://www.avma.org/KB/Resources/LiteratureReviews /Pages/Elephant-Training-Backgrounder.aspx.
4. Robert K. Greenleaf Center for Servant Leadership, https://www .greenleaf.org.
5. The Academy of Contemplative and Ethical Leadership, http://www .mindlifeinstitute.org.
6. Rodney Page (director, Flint Animal Cancer Center at Colorado State University College of Veterinary Medicine and Biomedical Sciences), email to Donald F. Smith, October 30, 15.
7. Nicholas Kristoff, "Evangelicals Without Blowhards," *New York Times*, July 30, 2011, http://www.nytimes.com/2011/07/31/opinion/sunday/kristof -evangelicals-without-blowhards.html.
8. Nicholas Kristoff, "Learning from the Sin of Sodom," *New York Times* Feb 28, 2010, http://www.nytimes.com/2010/02/28/opinion/28kristof.html.
9. Nicholas Kristoff, "A Little Respect for Dr. Foster," *New York Times*, March 29, 2015, http://www.nytimes.com/2015/03/29/opinion/sunday/nicholas -kristof-a-little-respect-for-dr-foster.html.

Epilogue

Secretary for One Health, *Reuters*
April 14, 2031

WASHINGTON—President Alicia Rodriguez announced this morning in a Rose Garden ceremony that Connie Lee, dean of the College of Veterinary Medicine at Johns Hopkins University, has been nominated as the inaugural Secretary of One Health. In yet another twist to what appears to be Rodriguez's crusade to unify the health sciences under the broad umbrella of humans, animals, and the environment, the president followed through on her commitment to appoint a veterinarian to the post.

Senator Clifford Reid, chair of the powerful Health and Human Services Committee, wasted no time in pledging to squelch the nomination. Standing on the steps outside the Senate chamber he promised to kill the appointment in committee. "Americans will not stand idly by as this president tries to have the future of our health dictated by some puppy doc, a lady vet at that," the senator barked.

The appointment of a veterinarian may not be as easily thwarted as Reid believes, however. Two months ago, Congress overwhelmingly passed and the president signed the One Health Bill. This legislation broadened the scope of research funding within the National Institutes of Health and Comparative Medicine, also creating the office of the Secretary of One Health. The cabinet-level post will oversee both the Department of Health and Human Services and the reconfigured United States Department of Agriculture, Agri-Food, and Environmental Security (formerly the USDA). Last month, the Congressional Health Care and Veterinary Caucuses also merged to form the Congressional One Health Caucus. All of these decisions were influenced strongly by the devastating impact of the recent phosphoserine transaminase (PSERT) outbreak that has left over 20,000 people permanently affected with idiopathic prion disease, commonly referred to as IPD, a debilitating neurological condition similar to mad cow disease.

During the announcement, the president deviated briefly from her prepared statement and spoke emphatically about the full scope of veterinary medicine. "If we are truly going to position veterinary medicine in its rightful place in promoting health for both people and animals, we need to once and for all embrace the reality that veterinarians are not just animal doctors, but have a unique understanding of comparative medicine and are critical members of our health care team," she said.

Addendum:

Dr. Lee was overwhelmingly confirmed as the new Secretary of One Health and served through for the remainder of Rodriguez's second term. Once in office, Lee built bridges across public and private institutions in health and other professions. As the capstone of her career, she catalyzed the formation of the Institute for Leadership in the Health Professions, a prominent think tank that promotes the full range of One Health opportunities, from zoonotic disease control and management to comparative medicine and the relatively new field of zooeyia.[1]

And veterinarians were never again referred to in public as "puppy docs."

A Flotilla of Medical, Agricultural, and Environmental Assistance
Greater Good Insights, *National Geographic Magazine*
July 1, 2026

What started four years ago as an innovative model of disaster relief in the developing world has become a futuristic prototype for programs as disparate as those run by the Bill & Melinda Gates Foundation and the International Committee of the Red Cross.

Project Compassion, the vision of five women who met at a leadership retreat in Lyons, Colorado, in the summer of 2022, is a merger of service and education that offers hope to some of the world's neediest regions. "It is servant-leadership taken to the next level," said Dr. Karen Stoufer, a retired senior executive with Christian Veterinary Mission who spent many years working in Nepal early in her career.

Led by veterinarian Mimi Stepanik, a graduate of UCLA College of Veterinary Medicine, and Naomi Perry, a lifelong veterinary technician, Project Compassion began as an idea born in the Rocky Mountains. Stepanik and Perry had been attending the Leadership in the Health Professions Institute retreat, created by Dr. Connie Lee, where people of all backgrounds learn from experts associated with the Global Fund, Peace Corps, Wharton School, and other institutions. One evening after a day of analyzing some of the top development and business models used in the countries where human and economic indicators are low, they went for a hike and were soon discussing whether women can change existing paradigms in solving the world's most challenging health and environmental issues.

"How is it," Stepanik mused, "that some of the most intractable challenges of hunger and disease in much of the world remain unsolved despite the investment of over $5 trillion in foreign assistance over the last two generations?" In countries that rank higher on the United Nations' Human Development Index (HDI), she added, we can now cure most cancers and treat obesity and heart disease. The average life span has been extended over ten years through manipulation of the genome, and the prevention and treatment of once entrenched problems is routine. "Even the common cold is a disease of antiquity," Stepanik said.

Yet when it comes to nations with lower HDIs (once sweepingly called *developing countries*), or when dealing with environmental and climate-related emergencies throughout the entire globe, Stepanik and Perry acknowledged that our response is still like that of the 1960s fire-engine veterinary practitioner rushing from crisis to crisis. As their trail conversation continued back at the ranch, so to speak, they were joined at the large common table by Dr. Phoebe Goldstein, a mid-career MD/MPH, and two venture capitalists, Chelsea Baker and Rachel Ortíz. Describing herself as the quintessential strategic risk taker, Baker said, "The two of us are a great team: I'm the one to put my foot in the water first, and Rachel here just dives in headlong." Ortíz shot her a smile.

"I love the thrill of risk-taking," Baker said, "but our company performs best when we consciously embrace the now proven leadership characteristics that have emerged since women have made up 30 percent of leaders in industry and government. Why don't we do the same now to tackle global disease and hunger?"

"Among all of us, we have the connections. We've built the relationships across the public and private spectrum," said Stepanik. Goldstein sat upright and noted, "Well then, now is the time to tap them."

Within six months, the five women had formed a team from the fields of health care, finance, and public policy, and they had appointed board cochairs who were former presidents of Harvard and the University of Chicago. Using a $1 billion start-up gift from a retired Oklahoma rancher, they purchased a retired Carnival Cruise Line ship. They tapped the pro bono services of supporters with expertise in everything from ocean-going navigation to engineering, anthropology to hydrology, and human health to veterinary medicine. The newly christened *Compassion I* set sail bearing flags from nations on every continent.

The first port of call was Nanjul in the tiny West African country of Gambia. An acute outbreak of contagious bovine pleuropneumonia, more virulent than the 2013 outbreak that had killed some 300,000 head of livestock, had devastated the cattle population and led to widespread starvation. Arriving in port, *Compassion I* quickly deployed emergency vaccination strategies. The intervention was a huge success, curtailing the outbreak and saving thousands, if not tens of thousands, of cattle. With its operating principle—"teach rather than do"—painted on the side of the ship, *Compassion I* left Gambia and headed for the next crisis in the making.

Now its third year, *Compassion I* has sailed to twelve different countries, setting up port in Asia, Africa, and the southern coast of the United States. The crew has worked with local health officials, learning from them about the most efficacious ways to teach rural populations everything from nutritional management of livestock to reducing antimicrobial residues in milk. To date, satellite clinics have been established in several countries. Local women, trained as veterinary technicians and nurses, are using these clinics to improve the health of cattle and goat herds as well as reduce rates of infant malnutrition and chronic diarrhea. Diagnostics and treatment education are available both at regional clinics and using donated smart phones. Outreach workers receive educational credit toward higher education degrees. Veterinary and medical students who intern on *Compassion I* boost their skills in the medical and social aspects of One Health principles.

Next year, *Compassion II* will set sail from Brazil with a crew of veterinarians, doctors, indigenous leaders, and environmental experts. Rather than head out to sea, the ship will travel up the Amazon to work with communities whose human and animal health are being still devastated by deforestation despite reductions in the practice over the past decade. They will work with the Rainforest Agricultural Health Alliance, established fifteen years ago and led by a team of agronomists, conservationists, veterinarians, and physicians. The Alliance, which successfully eradicated the Zika virus in 2018, will partner with *Compassion II* to address the high prevalence of infant mortality and chronic childhood diseases.

"It all started on a trail in Colorado," said Stepanik. "If I hadn't signed up for the Leadership in the Health Professions Institute Retreat, the five of us might not have had the chance to meet and dream up the vision of a floating outreach mission." Fortunate for the world, the five did what women do best: dream big, reach across borders, and get things done.

Prescience or prattle? You decide!

The future of veterinary medicine has not been written, and it is ours to imagine and ours to create. Though the new veterinary world requires many kinds of leadership, the common threads woven by female leaders are the humility to be mentored, the confidence to be flexible, the freedom to be innovative, and the patience to be persistent. Whether such leaders are visionary executives who follow heart-pounding routes of high risk or are women humbly pouring the vessels of their lives into others so they, in turn, may live more abundantly, there is a future role for everyone who has the will to become involved.

In the early months of 2013 when we began investigating the impact of women in the profession, some said the growth of women in leadership was on target, proceeding incrementally in its own time. All we needed was the already strong representation of women to progress through the system, and we would reach a natural tipping point. Or, as some would say with a twinkle in their eyes, "It will all work out; just wait until the men die off."

However, with all due respect to natural progression, we are convinced that change must be pushed forward. The transition will be accelerated by providing resources for women to better understand and address cultural, economic, and personal challenges as well as opportunities. Other initiatives will demand organizational and structural changes throughout the profession, including academia, where some of the most entrenched norms prevent substantive change.

We assert with absolute confidence that promoting women's leadership is not just the right thing to do; it's the wise thing to do. It's not just good for women individually or collectively; it's good for all of us in veterinary medicine. Most importantly, it is good for society, and that credo represents the very essence of this magnificent profession.

Notes

1.   Kate Hodgson, Louisa Barton, Marcia Darling, Florence A Kim, and Alan Monavvari, "Pets' Impact on Your Patients' Health: Leveraging Benefits and Mitigating Risk," *Journal of the American Board of Family Medicine* 28, no. 4 (2015): 526–34, http://www.jabfm.org/content/28/4/526.full; Kate Hodgson and Marcia Darling, "Zooeyia: An Essential Component of One Health," *The Canadian Veterinary Journal* 52, no. 2 (2011): 189–91, http://www.ncbi.nlm.nih.gov/pmc/articles/PMC3022463/.

Bibliography

Academy of Contemplative and Ethical Leadership. http://www.mindlifeinstitute.org.

Allen, Tammy D., Lisa M. Finkelstein, and Mark L. Poteet. *Designing Workplace Mentoring Programs: An Evidence-Based Approach*. Chichester, UK: Wiley-Blackwell, 2009.

Association of American Veterinary Medical Colleges. "Annual Data Report, 2015–2016." http://www.aavmc.org/data/images/research/aavmc%20data%20reports/2016%20aavmc%20public%20data%20-%20feb2516.pdf#page=9.

———. "Recruitment." http://www.aavmc.org/Programs-and-Initiatives/Recruitment.aspx.

Astin, Helen S., and Carole Leland. *Women of Influence, Women of Vision: A Cross-Generational Study of Leaders and Social Change*. San Francisco: Jossey-Bass, 1991.

Ayanna, Ariel Meysam. "Aggressive Parental Leave Incentivizing: A Statutory Proposal Toward Gender Equalization in the Workplace." *University of Pennsylvania Journal of Business Law* 293 (2007): 293–324. http://scholarship.law.upenn.edu/jbl/vol9/iss2/2.

Babcock, Linda, and Sara Laschever. *Women Don't Ask: The High Cost of Avoiding Negotiation—and Positive Strategies for Change*. New York: Princeton University Press, 2003.

Bacal, Jessica. *Mistakes I Made at Work: 25 Influential Women Reflect on What They Got Out of Getting It Wrong*. New York: Plume, 2014.

Bardwick, Judith M. "The Seasons of a Women's Life." In *Women's Lives: New Theory, Research and Policy*, edited by Dorothy G. McGuigan, 35–37. Ann Arbor: University of Michigan, 1980.

Bradley, Karen M., Elizabeth M. Charles, and Joan C. Hendricks. "A Renewed Call for Veterinary Leaders." *Journal of the American Veterinary Medical Association* 247, no. 6 (2015): 592–94. http://dx.doi.org/10.2460/javma.247.6.592.

Brooks, Alison Wood, and Francesca Gino. "Explaining Gender Differences at the Top." *Harvard Business Review*, September 23, 2015. https://hbr.org/2015/09/explaining-gender-differences-at-the-top.

Burns, Katie. "Taking the Leap: AVMA, Virginia-Maryland Center Among Groups Helping Veterinarians with Career Transitions." *Journal of the American Veterinary Medical Association News*. June 17, 2015. https://www .avma.org/News/JAVMANews/Pages/150701a.aspx.

Cain, Susan. *Quiet: The Power of Introverts in a World that Can't Stop Talking.* New York: Broadway Books, 2013.

Clance, Pauline Rose, and Susanne Imes. "The Impostor Phenomenon in High Achieving Women: Dynamics and Therapeutic Intervention." *Psychotherapy Theory, Research and Practice* 15, no. 3 (1978): 241–47.

Clapp, Edward P. "Omni-Directional Mentorship: Redefining Mentorship as a Reciprocal Process of Teaching and Learning." Mentorship Conference. Albuquerque: University of New Mexico, 2011. http://scholar.harvard .edu/edwardclapp/publications/omni-directional-mentorship-redefining -mentorship-reciprocal-process.

Crittenden, Ann. *The Price of Motherhood.* New York: Henry Holt and Company, 2001.

Crittenton Women's Union. "Massachusetts Economic Independence Index." March 2013. http://www.liveworkthrive.org/research_and_tools/reports _and_publications/Massachusetts_Economic_Independence_Index_2013.

Cummins, Denise. "Do You Feel Like an Impostor?" *Psychology Today*, October 3, 2013. https://www.psychologytoday.com/blog/good-thinking/201310 /do-you-feel-impostor.

Deutch, Claudia H. "Behind the Exodus of Executive Women: Boredom." *New York Times*, May 1, 2005. http://www.nytimes.com/2005/05/01/business /yourmoney/behind-the-exodus-of-executive-women-boredom.html.

Dicks, Michael R., Ross Knippenberg, Bridgette Bain, and Lisa Greenhill. *2015 AVMA Report on the Market for Veterinary Education.* October 2015. http:// dx.doi.org/10.13140/RG.2.1.3797.8003.

Doyle, Mary K. *Mentoring Heroes: 52 Fabulous Women's Paths to Success and the Mentors Who Empowered Them.* Batavia, IL: 3E Press, 2000.

Eagly, Alice H., and Linda L. Carli. *Through the Labyrinth: The Truth About How Women Become Leaders.* Boston: Harvard Business School Press, 2007.

Folbre, Nancy. *The Invisible Heart: Economics and Family Values.* New York: New Press, 2001.

Gallos, Joan V. "Exploring Women's Development: Implications for Career, Theory, Practice and Research." In *Handbook of Career Theory*, edited by Michael B. Arthur, Douglas T. Hall, and Barbara S. Lawrence, 110–32. New York: Cambridge University Press, 1996.

Gates, Ryan. "How to Figure Out What to Pay an Associate Veterinarian: Don't Skimp—You Want This Asset to Feel Valued." *DVM360*, October 1, 2014. http://veterinarybusiness.dvm360.com/figuring-out-what-pay-associate -veterinarian.

Giang, Vivian. "You Should Plan on Switching Careers Every Three Years for the Rest of Your Life." *Fast Company*, January 7, 2016. https://www.fastcompany .com/3055035/the-future-of-work/you-should-plan-on-switching-jobs-every -three-years-for-the-rest-of-your-.

Gilligan, Carol. "In a Different Voice: Women's Conception of the Self and of Morality." *Harvard Educational Review* 47, no. 4 (1978): 481–517.

Goleman, Daniel. "Social Chameleons May Pay Emotional Price." *New York Times*, March 12, 1985.

Greenleaf, Robert K. *Servant Leadership*. Mahwah, NJ: Paulist Press, 1977.

Hales, Dianna. *Just Like a Woman: How Gender Science is Redefining What Makes Us Female*. New York: Bantam, 1999.

Hodgson, Kate, Louisa Barton, Marcia Darling, Florence A Kim, and Alan Monavvari. "Pets' Impact on Your Patients' Health: Leveraging Benefits and Mitigating Risk." *Journal of the American Board of Family Medicine* 28, no. 4 (2015): 435–37. http://dx.doi.org/10.3122/jabfm.2015.04.140254.

———, and Marcia Darling. "Zooeyia: An Essential Component of One Health." *The Canadian Veterinary Journal* 52, no. 2 (2011): 526–34. http://www.ncbi .nlm.nih.gov/pmc/articles/PMC3022463/.

Ibarra, Herminia. "You're Never Too Old to Fake It 'Til You Make It." *Harvard Business Review*, January 8, 2015. https://hbr.org/2015/01/youre-never-too -experienced-to-fake-it-till-you-learn-it.

Irvine, Leslie, and Jenny R. Vermilya. "Gender Work in a Feminized Profession: The Case of Veterinary Medicine." *Gender and Society* 24, no. 1 (2010): 56–82. http://dx.doi.org/10.1177/0891243209355978.

Kay, Katty, and Claire Shipman. *The Confidence Code: The Art and Science of Self-Assurance—What Women Should Know*. New York: HarperBusiness, 2014.

Kellerman, Barbara, and Deborah L. Rhode. *Women and Leadership: The State of Play and Strategies for Change*. San Francisco: Wiley and Sons, 2007.

Kickul, Jill, and Norris Krueger. "Toward a New Model of Intentions: The Complexity of Gender, Cognitive Style, Culture, Social Norms, and Intensity on the Pathway to Entrepreneurship." Center for Gender in Organizations Simmons School of Management. http://www.simmons.edu/about-simmons /centers-organizations-and-institutes/cgo/publications/cgo-working-papers.

Kogan, Lori R., Sherry L. McConnell, and Regina Schoenfeld-Tacher. "Gender Differences and the Definition of Success: Male and Female Veterinary Students' Career and Work Performance Expectations." *Journal of Veterinary Medical Education* 31, no. 2 (2004): 154–60. http://dx.doi.org/10.3138 /jvme.31.2.154.

Kristoff, Nicholas. "A Little Respect for Dr. Foster." *New York Times*, March 29, 2015. http://www.nytimes.com/2015/03/29/opinion/sunday/nicholas-kristof -a-little-respect-for-dr-foster.html.

———. "Evangelicals Without Blowhards." *New York Times*, July 30, 2011. http:// www.nytimes.com/2011/07/31/opinion/sunday/kristof-evangelicals-without -blowhards.html.

———. "Learning from the Sin of Sodom." *New York Times*, February 28, 2010. http://www.nytimes.com/2010/02/28/opinion/28kristof.html.

Lloyd, James W., Lonnie J. King, Carol A. Mase, and Donna Harris. "Future Needs and Recommendations for Leadership in Veterinary Medicine." *Journal of the American Veterinary Medical Association* 226, no. 7 (2005): 1060–67. http://dx.doi.org/10.2460/javma.2005.226.1060.

Mainiero, Lisa, and Sherry Sullivan. *The Opt-Out Revolt: Why People Are Leaving Companies to Start Kaleidoscope Careers*. Boston: Nicholas Brealey America, 2006.

Miller, Claire Cane. "Men Do More at Home, But Not as Much as They Think." *New York Times*, November 12, 2015. http://www.nytimes.com/2015/11/12/upshot /men-do-more-at-home-but-not-as-much-as-they-think-they-do.html?_r=0.

Mills, Helen. "Can Entrepreneurship Be Taught?" *Canadian Woman Studies* 15, no. 1 (1994): 15–18.

National Research Council. *Workforce Needs in Veterinary Medicine*. Washington, DC: National Academies Press, 2011.

Parker, Patrick. "Change is Coming: What U.S. Colleges Must Do to Survive." *Wharton*, December 2, 2014. http://knowledge.wharton.upenn.edu/article /what-u-s-colleges-must-do-to-survive/.

Ravindran, Sandeep. "Feeling Like a Fraud: The Impostor Phenomenon in Science Writing." *The Open Notebook: The Stories Behind the Best Science Writing*, November 15, 2016. http://www.theopennotebook.com/2016/11/15/feeling -like-a-fraud-the-impostor-phenomenon-in-science-writing/.

"Revealing the Real Millennials: Career Expectations." *Catalyst.* July 13, 2015. http:// www.catalyst.org/knowledge/revealing-real-millennials-career-expectations.

Sandberg, Sheryl. *Lean In: Women, Work and the Will to Lead*. New York: Knopf, 2013.

Shen, Yaoqin, Ross Knippenberg, and Mike Dicks. "The Gender Wage Gap in Veterinary Medicine: Is Clinical Confidence a Factor?" *DVM360*, October 1, 2015. http://veterinarynews.dvm360.com/gender-wage-gap-veterinary -medicine-clinical-confidence-factor.

Slater, Margaret R., and Miriam Slater. "Women in Veterinary Medicine." *Journal of the American Veterinary Medical Association* 217, no. 4 (2000): 273–76. https://doi.org/10.2460/javma.2000.217.472.

Slaughter, Anne-Marie. "Why Women Still Can't Have It All." *Atlantic*, July 2012. http://www.theatlantic.com/magazine/archive/2012/07/why-women -still-cant-have-it-all/309020/.

Smith, Carin. "Gender and Work: What Veterinarians Can Learn from Research About Women, Men, and Work." *Journal of the American Veterinary Medical Association* 220, no. 9 (2002): 1304–11. https://doi.org/10.2460 /javma.2002.220.1304.

Smith, Donald F. "A Biography of and Interview with Joseph J. Merenda, DVM." https://ecommons.cornell.edu/bitstream/handle/1813/12877/Merenda,%20 Joseph%20J.%20'34%20BioInt.pdf?sequence=1.

"Social Entrepreneurship: Building the Field." *Ashoka Foundation*. https://www .ashoka.org/social_entrepreneur.

Stanford Distinguished Careers Institute. http://dci.stanford.edu.

Stone, Hal, and Sidra Stone. *Embracing Your Inner Critic: Turning Self-Criticism into a Creative Asset*. San Francisco: HarperOne, 1993.

Tannen, Deborah. *You Just Don't Understand: Women and Men in Conversation.* New York: Ballantine Publishing Group, 1990.

Townsend, Bickley. "Dissecting the Time Squeeze." *Cornell Employment and Family Careers Institute, Bronfenbrenner Life Course Center Issue Briefs* 3, no. 1 (2002): 1–4.

Vet Partners. http://www.vetpartners.org.

Young, Valerie. *The Secret Thoughts of Successful Women: Why Capable People Suffer from the Impostor Syndrome and How to Thrive in Spite of It.* New York: Crown Business, 2011.

Zachary, Lois J. *The Mentor's Guide: Facilitating Effective Learning Relationships.* San Francisco: Jossey-Bass, 2011.

Zerzan, Judy T., Rachel Hess, Ellen Schur, Russell S. Phillips, and Nancy Rigotti. "Making the Most of Mentors: A Guide for Mentees." *Academic Medicine* 84, no. 1 (2009): 140–44. https://doi.org/10.1097/ACM.0b013e3181906e8f.

Suggested Reading

Ashford, Susan. "Championing Charged Issues: The Case of Gender Equity Within Organizations." *Power and Influence in Organizations,* Edited by Roderick M. Kramer and Margaret A. Neale. Thousand Oaks, CA: Sage Publications, 1998.

Austin, Linda. *What's Holding You Back? 8 Critical Choices for Women's Success.* New York: Basic Books, 2000.

Barsh, Joanna, and Susie Cranston. *How Remarkable Women Lead: The Breakthrough Model for Work and Life.* New York: Crown Business, 2011.

Bellstrom, Kristen. "More Than Half of MBAs Say They Will Put Family Before Career." *Fortune,* October 12, 2015. http://fortune.com/2015/10/12/mba-family-before-career-study/.

Bernhut, Stephen. "In Conversation with Rosabeth Moss Kanter, The Professor as Business Leader." *Ivey Business Journal,* March/April 2006. http://iveybusinessjournal.com/publication/in-conversation-rosabeth-moss-kanter/.

Bristol, David G. "Gender Differences in Salary and Practice Ownership Expectations of Matriculating Veterinary Students." *Journal of the American*

Veterinary Medical Association 239, no. 3 (2011): 329–34. http://dx.doi.org/10.2460/javma.239.3.329.

Carroll, Susan J. *The Impact of Women in Public Office* Bloomington: Indiana University Press, 2001.

Catalyst. "Women in Academia." July 9, 2015. http://www.catalyst.org/knowledge/women-academia.

Cutting, Gary, and Nancy Fraser. "A Feminism Where 'Lean In' Means Leaning On Others." *New York Times*, October 15, 2015. http://opinionator.blogs.nytimes.com/2015/10/15/a-feminism-where-leaning-in-means-leaning-on-others/.

Daniell, Ellen. *Every Other Thursday: Stories and Strategies from Successful Women Scientists.* New Haven, CT: Yale University Press, 2006.

Dittman, Melissa. "Generational Differences at Work: A Psychologist Studies Ways to Help Traditionalists, Baby Boomers, Gen Xers and Millennials Work Better Together, Despite Their Generational Differences." *American Psychological Association* 36, no. 6 (2005): 54.

Dittmar, Kelly. "The Gender Gap: Gender Differences in Vote Choices and Political Orientations." Center for American Women in Politics, Rutgers University, July 15, 2014. http://www.cawp.rutgers.edu/sites/default/files/resources/closerlook_gender-gap-07-15-14.pdf.

Greenhill, Lisa M., Kauline Cipriani Davis, Patricia M. Lowrie, and Sandra F. Amass. *Navigating Diversity and Inclusion in Veterinary Medicine.* West Lafayette, IN: Purdue University Press, 2013.

Jacobs, Jerry A., and Kathleen Gerson. "Do Americans Feel Overworked? Comparing Actual and Ideal Working Time." *Work and Family: Research Informing Policy*, Edited by Toby I. Parcel and Daniel B. Cornfield. Thousand Oaks, CA: Sage Publications, 2000.

Kellerman, Barbara. *Hard Times: Leadership in America.* Redwood City, CA: Stanford University Press, 2015.

Kokalitcheva, Kia. "Joyus' CEO Has a New Plan to Get More Women onto Startup Boards." *Fortune*, July 15, 2015. http://fortune.com/2015/07/15/joyus-ceo-diversity-board/.

Kolb, Deborah. "Negotiation Through a Gender Lens." Center for Gender in Organizations Simmons School of Management, September 2002. http://

www.simmons.edu/about-simmons/centers-organizations-and-institutes/cgo
/publications/cgo-working-papers.

———, and Judith Williams. *The Shadow Negotiation: How Women Can Master the Hidden Agendas that Determine Bargaining Success*. New York: Simon & Schuster, 2000.

Kouzes, James M., and Barry Z. Posner. "Leadership Begins With an Inner Journey." *Leader to Leader*. Hoboken, NJ: John Wiley and Sons, 2003.

Kurtz, Suzanne. "Teaching Learning and Communication in Veterinary Medicine." *Journal of Veterinary Medical Education* 33, no. 1 (2006): 11–19. http://dx.doi.org/10.3138/jvme.33.1.11.

Lawless, Jennifer, and Richard L. Fox. *It Takes a Candidate: Why Women Don't Run for Office*. Cambridge, UK: Cambridge University Press, 2005.

Lincoln, Anne E. "The Shifting Supply of Men and Women to Occupations: Feminization in Veterinary Education." *Social Forces* 88, no. 5 (2010): 1969–98.

Marek, Kiersten, and David Callahan. "Heft or Hype: How Much Do Women Leaders in Philanthropy Really Matter?" *Inside Philanthropy*, March 25, 2015. http://www.insidephilanthropy.com/home/2016/3/25/heft-or-hype -how-much-do-women-leaders-in-philanthropy-reall.html#.

———. "What You Need to Know If You're an Academic and Want to be a Mom." *New York Times*, July 16, 2013. http://www.nytimes.com /roomfordebate/2013/07/08/should-women-delay-motherhood/what-you -need-to-know-if-youre-an-academic-and-want-to-be-a-mom.

Mason, Mary Ann, and Marc Goulden. "Marriage and Baby Blues: Redefining Gender Equity in the Academy." *Annals of the American Academy of Political and Social Science* 596 (2004): 86–103.

McGregor, Lindsay, and Neel Doshi. "Why It Doesn't Take a NonProfit Career To Make A Difference." *Fast Company*, November 18, 2015. http://www .fastcompany.com/3053650/know-it-all/why-it-doesnt-take-a-nonprofit -career-to-make-a-difference-at-work.

McKinsey Global Institute Report. *Women Matter: The Business and Economic Case for Gender Diversity*. http://www.mckinsey.com/global-themes/women-matter.

Meyerson, Debra. *Tempered Radicals: How People Use Difference to Inspire Change at Work*. Boston: Harvard Business School Publishing, 2001.

Monosson, Emily. *Motherhood, The Elephant in the Laboratory, Women Scientists Speak Out*. Ithaca, NY: Cornell University Press, 2008.

Moravscik, Andrew. "Why I Put My Wife's Career First." *Atlantic Monthly*, October 2015. http://www.theatlantic.com/magazine/archive/2015/10/why -i-put-my-wifes-career-first/403240/.

Nicholson, Emily. "Accounting for Career Breaks." *Science* 348 no. 6236 (2015): 830. http://dx.doi.org/10.1126/science.348.6236.830.

O'Reilly, Nancy D. *Leading Women: 20 Influential Women Share Their Secrets to Leadership, Business and Life*. Avon, MA: Adams Media, 2015.

PayScale. "Inside the Gender Pay Gap." http://www.payscale.com/data-packages /gender-pay-gap.

Popova, Maria. "David Whyte on How to Break the Tyranny of Work/Life Balance." *Brainpickings*. https://www.brainpickings.org/2015/03/11/david -whyte-three-marriages-work-life/.

Rezvani, Selena. *Pushback: How Smart Women Ask and Stand Up for What They Want*. San Francisco: Jossey-Bass, 2015.

Sanbonmatsu, Kira. "Why Women? The Impact of Women in Elective Office." *Political Parity*. https://www.politicalparity.org/wp-content/uploads/2015/08 /Parity-Research-Women-Impact.pdf.

Shell, G. Richard. *Bargaining for Advantage: Negotiation Strategies for Reasonable People*. Westminster, UK: Penguin Books, 2006.

Slaughter, Anne-Marie. *Unfinished Business: Women Men Work Family*. New York: Random House, 2015.

Smola, Karen Wey, and Charlotte C. Sutton. "Generational Differences: Revisiting Generational Work Values for the New Millennium." *Journal of Organizational Behavior* 23, no. 4 (2002): 363–82.

Taylor, Karen Ann, and Daniel C. Robinson. "Unleashing the Potential: Women's Development and Ways of Knowing as a Perspective for Veterinary Medical Education." *Journal of Veterinary Medical Education* 43, no. 4 (2009): 135–44. http://dx.doi.org/10.3138/jvme.36.1.135.

Valdata, Patricia. "The Ticking of the Biological and Tenure Clocks: Princeton University Institutes New Policy, Placing the School at the Forefront of Family-Friendly Workplaces." *Diverse Issues in Higher Education* 17 (2005): 34.

Whyte, David. *The Three Marriages: Reimagining Work, Self and Relationship*. New York: Riverhead Books, 2009.

Yavorsky, Jill E., Claire M. Kamp Dush, and Sarah J. Schoppe-Sullivan. "The Production of Inequality: The Gender Division of Labor Across the

Transition to Parenthood." *Journal of Marriage and Family* 77, no. 3 (2015): 662–79. http://dx.doi.org/10.1111/jomf.12189.

Zenger, Jack, and Josheph Folkman. "Are Women Better Leaders Than Men." *Harvard Business Review*, March 15, 2012. https://hbr.org/2012/03/a-study -in-leadership-women-do.

Index

About the Authors

Julie Kumble, M.Ed.

Julie Kumble is a researcher, writer, and director in women's leadership, and was the founding director of a leadership training program called the Leadership Institute for Political and Public Impact, which she developed at the Women's Fund of Western Massachusetts. She has been a US State Department Fellow, recipient of the International Women's Day Award from the Amherst League of Women Voters, grantee of the Foundation for Motivated Women, and US Peace Corps volunteer. She is a founding director of the Women's Veterinary Leadership Development Initiative, and developed a course on women's leadership in veterinary medicine, which debuted in March 2014 at Cornell University and subsequently was offered at other veterinary colleges.

Donald F. Smith, DVM, DACVS

Dr. Donald F. Smith served as the ninth dean of Cornell University's College of Veterinary Medicine. An accomplished large animal surgeon and an avid veterinary historian, Smith's digital collection of first-person interviews with veterinarians who began their careers during the 1930s and 1940s is a national veterinary treasure, and his popular blog at www.veritasdvmblog.com attracts readers from around the world. His commissioned book on the fiftieth anniversary of the Association of American Veterinary Medical Colleges, *Pathways to Progress*, was released to wide acclaim in 2016. Smith was a diplomate of the American College of Veterinary Surgeons and a member of the National Academy of Practices. He passed away on October 29, 2016.